R. U. R.

THE INSECT PLAY

R. U. R.

and

THE
INSECT PLAY

by
THE BROTHERS ČAPEK

Oxford   New York

OXFORD UNIVERSITY PRESS

Oxford University Press Walton Street, Oxford OX2 6DP

Oxford New York Toronto
Petaling Jaya Singapore Hong Kong Tokyo
Delhi Bombay Calcutta Madras Karachi
Nairobi Dar es Salaam Cape Town
Melbourne Auckland

and associated companies in
Berlin Ibadan

Oxford is a trade mark of Oxford University Press

ISBN 0–19–281010–3

'R. U. R.' and 'The Insect Play' were first published as separate
editions in 1923 and were each reprinted ten times
This edition first issued as an Oxford University Press paperback 1961
Thirteenth impression 1989

Printed in Great Britain by
The Guernsey Press Co. Ltd.
Guernsey, Channel Islands

CONTENTS

R. U. R.

(ROSSUM'S UNIVERSAL ROBOTS)

A Play

in three acts and an epilogue

by

KAREL ČAPEK

Translated from the Czech
by P. Selver and adapted for
the English stage by Nigel Playfair

For acting purposes it was found necessary to make a few alterations not included in this version. Chief of these was the removal from the list of characters of two names, FABRY and HELMAN.

R. U. R. was first produced by Mr. BASIL DEAN for the 'REANDEAN' Company, at the ST. MARTIN'S THEATRE, in April 1923.

SCENES

CHARACTERS

HARRY DOMAIN, *General Manager for Rossum's Universal Robots*

FABRY, *Chief Engineer for R. U. R.*

DR. GALL, *Head of the Physiological Department, R. U. R.*

DR. HELMAN, *Psychologist-in-Chief*

JACOB BERMAN, *Managing Director, R. U. R.*

ALQUIST, *Clerk of the Works, R. U. R.*

HELENA GLORY, *Daughter of Professor Glory, of Oxbridge University*

EMMA, *Her Maid*

MARIUS, *A Robot*

SULLA, *A Robotess*

RADIUS, *A Robot*

PRIMUS, *A Robot*

HELENA, *A Robotess*

A ROBOT SERVANT and numerous Robots
ON A REMOTE ISLAND

Male fantasy —
reproduction without sex?

ACT I

Central office of the factory of ROSSUM'S UNIVERSAL
ROBOTS. *Entrance at the back on the right. The windows look
out on to endless rows of factory buildings.* DOMAIN *is sitting in
a revolving chair at a large 'knee-hole' writing-table on which stand
an electric lamp, telephone, letter-weight, correspondence-file, etc.
On the left-hand wall hang large maps showing steamship and
railway routes, a large calendar, and a clock indicating a few
minutes before noon. On the right-hand wall are fastened printed
placards:* 'CHEAP LABOUR. ROSSUM'S ROBOTS.'
'ROBOTS FOR THE TROPICS. 150 DOLLARS EACH.'
'EVERY ONE SHOULD BUY HIS OWN ROBOT 'DO YOU
WANT TO CHEAPEN YOUR OUTPUT? ORDER ROSSUM'S
ROBOTS': *more maps, shipping transport arrangements, etc. A
tape-machine showing rates of exchange stands in one corner. In
contrast to these wall fittings the floor is covered with a splendid
Turkey carpet. On the right stand a round table, a sofa, leather
arm-chair, and a bookshelf containing bottles of wine and spirits
instead of books. Cashier's desk on the left. Next to* DOMAIN'S
table SULLA *is typing letters.*

DOMAIN. [*Dictating*] 'We do not accept any liability for
goods damaged in transit. When the consignment was
shipped, we drew your Captain's attention to the fact
that the vessel was unsuitable for the transport of
Robots. The matter is one for your own Insurance
Company. We beg to remain, for Rossum's Universal
Robots——' Finished?

SULLA. Yes.

DOMAIN. Another letter. 'To the E. B. Hudson Agency,
New York. Date. We beg to acknowledge receipt of
order for five thousand Robots. As you are sending

I

your own vessel, please dispatch as cargo briquettes for R.U.R., the same to be credited as part-payment of the amount due to us. We beg to remain——' Finished?

SULLA. [*Typing the last word*] Yes.

DOMAIN. 'Friedrichswerke, Hamburg. Date. We beg to acknowledge receipt of order for fifteen thousand Robots.'

> [*The house telephone rings.* DOMAIN *picks it up and speaks into it*]

Hallo, this is the central office—yes—certainly. Oh yes, as usual. Of course, send them a cable. Good. [*Hangs up the telephone*] Where did I leave off?

SULLA. We beg to acknowledge receipt of order for fifteen thousand R.

DOMAIN. [*Thoughtfully*] Fifteen thousand R. Fifteen thousand R.

MARIUS. [*Entering*] There's a lady, sir, asking to——

DOMAIN. Who is she?

MARIUS. I don't know, sir. She gave me this card.

DOMAIN. [*Reads*] Professor William Glory, St. Trydeswyde's, Oxbridge—Ask her to come in.

MARIUS. [*Opening the door*] Please step this way, ma'am.

Enter HELENA GLORY

> [*Exit* MARIUS

DOMAIN. [*Standing up*] What can I do for you, madam?

HELENA. You are Mr. Domain, the general manager.

DOMAIN. I am.

HELENA. I have come to you——

DOMAIN. With Professor Glory's card. That is sufficient.

HELENA. Professor Glory is my father. I am Helena Glory.

DOMAIN. Miss Glory, it is an unusual honour for us—to be—to be——

HELENA. Yes—well.

DOMAIN. To be allowed to welcome the distinguished Professor's daughter. Please sit down. Sulla, you may go.   [*Exit* SULLA

[*Sitting down*] How can I be of service to you, Miss Glory?

HELENA. I have come here——

DOMAIN. To have a look at our factory where people are made. Like all visitors. Well, there's no objection.

HELENA. I thought it was forbidden——

DOMAIN. It is forbidden to enter the factory, of course. But everybody comes here with an introduction and then——

HELENA. And you show everybody——?

DOMAIN. Only certain things. The manufacture of artificial people is a secret process.

HELENA. If you only knew how enormously that——

DOMAIN. Interests me, you were going to say. Europe's talking about nothing else.

HELENA. Why don't you let me finish speaking?

DOMAIN. I beg your pardon. Did you want to say anything else?

HELENA. I only wanted to ask——

DOMAIN. Whether I could make a special exception in your case and show you our factory. Certainly, Miss Glory.

HELENA. How do you know that I wanted to ask you that?

DOMAIN. They all do. [*Standing up*] We shall consider it a special honour to show you more than the rest, because—indeed—I mean——

HELENA. Thank you.

DOMAIN. But you must undertake not to divulge the least——

HELENA. [*Standing up and giving him her hand*] My word of honour.

DOMAIN. Thank you. Won't you raise your veil?

HELENA. Oh, of course, you want to see me. I beg your pardon.

DOMAIN. What is it, please?

HELENA. Would you mind letting my hand go.

DOMAIN. [*Releasing it*] I beg your pardon.

HELENA. [*Taking off her veil*] You want to see whether I am a spy or not. How cautious you are!

DOMAIN. [*Looking at her intently*] H'm, of course—we—that is——

HELENA. You don't trust me?

DOMAIN. Oh, indeed, Miss Glory, I'm only too delighted. Weren't you lonely on the voyage?

HELENA. Why?

DOMAIN. Because—I mean to say—you're so young.

4

HELENA. Yes. Shall we go straight into the factory?

DOMAIN. Twenty-two, I think, eh?

HELENA. Twenty-two what?

DOMAIN. Years.

HELENA. Twenty-one. Why do you want to know?

DOMAIN. Because—as—[*With enthusiasm*] You'll make a long stay, won't you?

HELENA. That depends on how much of the factory you show me.

DOMAIN. Oh, hang the factory. But you shall see everything, Miss Glory, indeed you shall. Please sit down. Would you like to hear the story of the invention?

HELENA. Yes, please. [*Sits down.*]

DOMAIN. Well, then. [*Sits down on the writing-table, looks at* HELENA *with rapture, and reels off rapidly*] It was in the year 1922 that old Rossum the great physiologist, who was then quite a young scientist, betook himself to this distant island for the purpose of studying the ocean fauna, full stop. On this occasion he attempted by chemical synthesis to imitate the living matter known as protoplasm, until he suddenly discovered a substance which behaved exactly like living matter, although its chemical composition was different; that was in the year 1932, exactly four hundred years after the discovery of America, whew!

HELENA. Do you know that by heart?

DOMAIN. Yes. Physiology, Miss Glory, is not my line. Shall I go on?

HELENA. Please do.

5

DOMAIN. [*Solemnly*] And then, Miss Glory, old Rossum wrote the following in his day book: 'Nature has found only one method of organizing living matter. There is, however, another method more simple, flexible, and rapid, which has not yet occurred to nature at all. This second process by which life can be developed was discovered by me today.' Imagine him, Miss Glory, writing those wonderful words. Imagine him sitting over a test-tube and thinking how the whole tree of life would grow from it, how all animals would proceed from it, beginning with some sort of beetle and ending with man himself. A man of different substance from ours. Miss Glory, that was a tremendous moment.

HELENA. Go on, please.

DOMAIN. Now the thing was, how to get the life out of the test-tube and hasten development: to form organs, bones and nerves, and so on: to find such substances as catalytics, enzymes, hormones, and so forth, in short— you understand?

HELENA. I don't know. Not much, I'm afraid.

DOMAIN. Never mind. You see, with the help of his tinctures he could make whatever he wanted. He could have produced a Medusa with the brain of a Socrates or a worm fifty yards long. But being without a grain of humour, he took it into his head to make a normal vertebrate. This artificial living matter of his had a raging thirst for life. It didn't mind being sewn up or mixed together. *That*, you'll admit, couldn't be done with natural albumen. And that's how he set about it.

HELENA. About what?

DOMAIN. About imitating nature. First of all he tried making an artificial dog. That took him several years and resulted in a sort of stunted calf which died in a

6

few days. I'll show it you in the museum. And then old Rossum started on the manufacture of man.   [*Pause*

HELENA. And I must divulge this to nobody?

DOMAIN. To nobody in the world.

HELENA. It's a pity that it can already be found in every school lesson book.

DOMAIN. Yes. [*Jumps up from the table and sits down beside* HELENA] But do you know what isn't in the lesson books? [*Taps his forehead*] That old Rossum was quite mad. Seriously, Miss Glory, you must keep this to yourself. The old crank actually wanted to make people.

HELENA. But you do make people.

DOMAIN. Synthetically, Miss Helena. But old Rossum meant it actually. He wanted to become a sort of scientific substitute for God, you know. He was a fearful materialist, and that's why he did it all. His sole purpose was nothing more or less than to supply proof that Providence was no longer necessary. So he took it into his head to make people exactly like us. Do you know anything about anatomy?

HELENA. Only a very little.

DOMAIN. So do I. Imagine then that he decided to manufacture everything as in the human body. I'll show you in the museum the bungling attempt it took him ten years to produce. It was to have been a man, but it lived for three days only. Then up came young Rossum, an engineer, the nephew of old Rossum. A wonderful fellow, Miss Glory. When he saw what a mess of it the old man was making, he said: 'It's absurd to spend ten years making a man. If you can't make him quicker than nature, you may as well shut up shop.' Then he set about learning anatomy himself.

7

Man v working machines

HELENA. There's nothing about that in the lesson books.

DOMAIN. [*Standing up*] The lesson books are full of paid advertisement, and rubbish at that. For example, it says there that the Robots were invented by an old man. But it was young Rossum who had the idea of making living and intelligent working machines. What the lesson books say about the united efforts of the two great Rossums is all a fairy tale. They used to have dreadful rows. The old atheist hadn't the slightest conception of industrial matters, and the end of it was that young Rossum shut him up in some laboratory or other and let him fritter the time away with his monstrosities, while he himself started on the business from an engineer's point of view. Old Rossum cursed him, and before he died he managed to botch up two physiological horrors. Then one day they found him dead in the laboratory. That's the whole story.

HELENA. And what about the young man?

DOMAIN. Well, any one who's looked into anatomy will have seen at once that man is too complicated, and that a good engineer could make him more simply. So young Rossum began to overhaul anatomy and tried to see what could be left out or simplified. In short——but this isn't boring you, Miss Glory?

HELENA. No; on the contrary, it's awfully interesting.

DOMAIN. So young Rossum said to himself: A man is something that, for instance, feels happy, plays the fiddle, likes going for walks, and, in fact, wants to do a whole lot of things that are really unnecessary.

HELENA. Oh!

DOMAIN. Wait a bit. That are unnecessary when he's wanted, let us say, to weave or to count. Do you play the fiddle?

8

HELENA. No.

DOMAIN. That's a pity. But a working machine must not want to play the fiddle, must not feel happy, must not do a whole lot of other things. A petrol motor must not have tassels or ornaments, Miss Glory. And to manufacture artificial workers is the same thing as to manufacture motors. The process must be of the simplest, and the product of the best from a practical point of view. What sort of worker do you think is the best from a practical point of view?

HELENA. The best? Perhaps the one who is most honest and hard-working.

DOMAIN. No, the cheapest. The one whose needs are the smallest. Young Rossum invented a worker with the minimum amount of requirements. He had to simplify him. He rejected everything that did not contribute directly to the progress of work. In this way he rejected everything that makes man more expensive. In fact, he rejected man and made the Robot. My dear Miss Glory, the Robots are not people. Mechanically they are more perfect than we are, they have an enormously developed intelligence, but they have no soul. Have you ever seen what a Robot looks like inside?

HELENA. Good gracious, no!

DOMAIN. Very neat, very simple. Really a beautiful piece of work. Not much in it, but everything in flawless order. The product of an engineer is technically at a higher pitch of perfection than a product of nature.

HELENA. Man is supposed to be the product of nature.

DOMAIN. So much the worse. Nature hasn't the least notion of modern engineering. Would you believe that young Rossum played at being nature?

9

HELENA. What do you mean?

DOMAIN. He began to manufacture Super-Robots—regular giants. He tried to make them four yards high. But they were a frost.

HELENA. A frost?

DOMAIN. Yes. For no reason at all their limbs used to keep snapping off. Evidently our planet is too small for giants. Now we only make Robots of normal size and of very high-class human finish.

HELENA. I saw the first Robots at home. The town council bought them—I mean engaged them for work.

DOMAIN. Bought them, dear Miss Glory. Robots are bought and sold.

HELENA. These were employed as sweepers. I saw them sweeping. They are so strange and quiet.

DOMAIN. Did you see my typist?

HELENA. I didn't notice her particularly.

DOMAIN. [*Rings*] You see, Rossum's Universal Robot factory don't produce a uniform brand of Robots. We have Robots of finer and coarser grades. The best will live about twenty years.

HELENA. Then they perish?

DOMAIN. Yes, they get used up.

Enter SULLA

DOMAIN. Sulla, let Miss Glory look at you.

HELENA. [*Standing up and holding out her hand*] So glad to meet you. You must feel terribly dull in this out-of-the-way spot, don't you?

SULLA. I don't know, Miss Glory. Please sit down.

HELENA. [*Sitting down*] Where do you come from?

SULLA. From there, from the factory.

HELENA. Ah, you were born there.

SULLA. Yes, I was made there.

HELENA. [*Jumping up*] What?

DOMAIN. [*Laughing*] Sulla is a Robot.

HELENA. Oh, I beg your pardon——

DOMAIN. [*Laying his hand on* SULLA's *shoulder*] Sulla isn't angry. See, Miss Glory, the kind of skin we make. Feel her face.

HELENA. Oh, no, no.

DOMAIN. You wouldn't know that she's of different material from us. Turn round, Sulla.

HELENA. Stop, stop!

DOMAIN. Talk to Miss Glory, Sulla. She's an important visitor.

SULLA. Please sit down. [*Both sit down.*] Did you have a pleasant crossing?

HELENA. Oh yes, certainly.

SULLA. Don't go back on the *Amelia*, Miss Glory. The barometer is falling steadily. Wait for the *Pennsylvania*. That's a very good powerful vessel.

DOMAIN. What's its speed?

SULLA. Twenty knots an hour. Twelve thousand tons. One of the latest vessels, Miss Glory.

HELENA. Tha—thank you.

SULLA. A crew of eighty, Captain Harpy, eight boil-
ers——

DOMAIN. [*Laughing*] That's enough, Sulla. Now show us
your knowledge of French.

HELENA. You know French?

SULLA. I know four languages. I can write: Dear Sir,
Monsieur, Geehrter Herr, Y Mustre Señor.

HELENA. [*Jumping up*] What nonsense! Sulla isn't a
Robot. Sulla is a girl like me. Sulla, it's naughty of you
—why do you take part in such a hoax?

SULLA. I am a Robot.

HELENA. No, no, you're not telling the truth. Oh, Sulla,
forgive me, I know—they've forced you to do it for an
advertisement. Sulla, you are a girl like me, aren't you?
Tell me, now.

DOMAIN. I'm sorry, Miss Glory. Sulla is a Robot.

HELENA. *You're* not telling the truth.

DOMAIN. [*Starting up*] What? [*Rings*] Excuse me, Miss
Glory, then I must convince you.

Enter MARIUS

DOMAIN. Marius, take Sulla into the testing-room for
them to open her. Quickly.

HELENA. Where?

DOMAIN. Into the testing-room. When they've cut her
up, you can go and have a look.

HELENA. I shan't go.

DOMAIN. Excuse me, you spoke of lies.

HELENA. You wouldn't have her killed?

DOMAIN. You can't kill machines.

HELENA. [*Embracing* SULLA] Don't be afraid, Sulla, I won't let you go. Tell me, darling, are they always so cruel to you? You mustn't put up with that, Sulla. You mustn't.

SULLA. I am a Robot.

HELENA. That doesn't matter. Robots are just as good as we are. Sulla, you wouldn't let yourself be cut to pieces.

SULLA. Yes.

HELENA. Oh, you're not afraid of death, then?

SULLA. I cannot tell, Miss Glory.

HELENA. Do you know what would happen to you there?

SULLA. Yes, I should cease to move.

HELENA. How dreadful.

DOMAIN. Marius, tell Miss Glory what you are.

MARIUS. Marius, the Robot.

DOMAIN. Would you take Sulla into the testing-room?

MARIUS. Yes.

DOMAIN. Would you be sorry for her?

MARIUS. I cannot tell.

DOMAIN. What would happen to her?

MARIUS. She would cease to move. They would put her into the stamping-mill.

DOMAIN. That is death, Marius. Aren't you afraid of death?

Robots = working class

MARIUS. No.

DOMAIN. You see, Miss Glory, the Robots are not at-tached to life. They have no reason to be. They have no enjoyments. They are less than so much grass.

HELENA. Oh, stop. Send them away.

DOMAIN. Marius, Sulla, you may go.

[*Exeunt* SULLA *and* MARIUS

HELENA. How terrible. It's scandalous!

DOMAIN. Why scandalous?

HELENA. It is, of course it is. Why did you call her Sulla?

DOMAIN. Isn't it a nice name?

HELENA. It's a man's name. Sulla was a Roman General.

DOMAIN. Oh, we thought that Marius and Sulla were lovers.

HELENA. No. Marius and Sulla were generals, and fought against each other in the year—I've forgotten now.

DOMAIN. Come here to the window. What do you see?

HELENA. Bricklayers.

DOMAIN. They are Robots. All our workpeople are Robots. And down there, can you see anything.

HELENA. Some sort of office.

DOMAIN. A counting-house. And in it——

HELENA. Clerks—a lot of clerks.

DOMAIN. They are Robots. All our clerks are Robots. When you see the factory——

[*Sound of factory whistles and sirens*

Midday. The Robots don't know when to stop work. In two hours I'll show you the kneading-trough.

HELENA. What kneading-trough?

DOMAIN. [*Dryly*] The pestles and mortar as it were for beating up the paste. In each one we mix the ingredients for a thousand Robots at one operation. Then there are the vats for the preparation of liver, brains, and so on. Then you'll see the bone factory. After that I'll show you the spinning-mill.

HELENA. What spinning-mill?

DOMAIN. For weaving nerves and veins. Miles and miles of digestive tubes pass through it at a stretch. Then there's the fitting-shed, where all the parts are put together, like motor-cars. Next comes the drying-kiln and the warehouse in which the new products work.

HELENA. Good gracious, do they have to work immediately?

DOMAIN. Well, you see, they work like any new appliance. They get used to existence. They sort of grow firm inside. We have to make a slight allowance for natural development. And in the meantime they undergo training.

HELENA. How is that done?

DOMAIN. It's much the same as going to school. They learn to speak, write, and count. They've astonishing memories, you know. If you were to read a twenty-volume Encyclopaedia to them, they'd repeat it all to you with absolute accuracy. But they never think of anything new. Then they're sorted out and distributed. Fifteen thousand daily, not counting a regular percentage of defective specimens which are thrown into the stamping-mill . . . and so on—and so on. Oh, let's

Enterprise
v
set

talk about something else. There's only a handful of us among a hundred thousand Robots, and not one woman. We talk about nothing but the factory, all day, every day. It's just as if we're under a curse, Miss Glory.

HELENA. I'm so sorry I said that—that—you weren't speaking the truth.

[*A knock at the door*

DOMAIN. Come in, boys.
   [*From the L. enter* MR. FABRY, DR. GALL, DR. HELMAN, ALQUIST]

DR. GALL. I beg your pardon, I hope we're not in the way.

DOMAIN. Come along in. Miss Glory, here are Mr. Alquist, Mr. Fabry, Dr. Gall, and Dr. Helman. This is Professor Glory's daughter.

HELENA. [*Embarrassed*] How do you do?

FABRY. We had no idea——

DR. GALL. Very honoured, I'm sure——

ALQUIST. Welcome, Miss Glory.
   [BERMAN *rushes in from the* R]

BERMAN. Hallo, what's up?

DOMAIN. Come in, Berman. This is Mr. Berman, Miss Glory. This is the daughter of Professor Glory.

HELENA. I'm very glad to meet you.

BERMAN. By Jove, that's splendid. Miss Glory, may we send a cablegram to the papers about your——

HELENA. No, no, please don't.

DOMAIN. Sit down, please, Miss Glory.

BERMAN. Allow me——

DR. GALL. [*Dragging up arm-chairs*] Please——

FABRY. Excuse me——

ALQUIST. What sort of a crossing did you have?

DR. GALL. Are you going to stay here long?

FABRY. What do you think of the factory, Miss Glory?

HELMAN. Did you come over on the *Amelia*?

DOMAIN. Be quiet, let Miss Glory speak.

HELENA. [*To* DOMAIN] What am I to speak to them about?

DOMAIN. [*Surprised*] About what you like.

HELENA. Shall . . . may I speak quite frankly?

DOMAIN. Why, of course.

HELENA. [*Wavering, then with desperate resolution*] Tell me, doesn't it ever distress you to be treated like this?

FABRY. Treated?—Who by?

HELENA. Everybody.
    [*All look at each other in consternation*]

ALQUIST. Treated?

DR. GALL. What makes you think that?

HELMAN. Treated?

BERMAN. Really!

HELENA. Don't you feel that you might be living a better life?

DR. GALL. Well, that depends what you mean, Miss Glory.

HELENA. I mean that—[*Bursting out*] that it's perfectly

outrageous. It's terrible. [*Standing up*] The whole of Europe is talking about how you're being treated. That's why I came here to see, and it's a thousand times worse than could have been imagined. How can you put up with it?

ALQUIST. Put up with what?

HELENA. Your position here. Good heavens, you are living creatures just like us, like the whole of Europe, like the whole world. It's scandalous, disgraceful!

BERMAN. Good gracious, Miss Glory.

FABRY. Well, boys, she's not so far out. We live here just like Red Indians.

HELENA. Worse than Red Indians. May, oh, may I call you brothers.

BERMAN. Of course you may, why not?

HELENA. Brothers, I have not come here as my father's daughter. I have come on behalf of the Humanity League. Brothers, the Humanity League now has over two hundred thousand members. Two hundred thousand people are on your side and offer you their help.

BERMAN. Two hundred thousand people, that's quite a tidy lot, Miss Glory, quite good.

FABRY. I'm always telling you there's nothing like good old Europe. You see, they've not forgotten us. They're offering us help.

DR. GALL. What help? A theatre?

HELMAN. An orchestra?

HELENA. More than that.

ALQUIST. Just you?

HELENA. Oh, never mind about me. I'll stay as long as is necessary.

BERMAN. By Jove, that's good.

ALQUIST. Domain, I'm going to get the best room ready for Miss Glory.

DOMAIN. Wait a moment. I'm afraid that—that Miss Glory hasn't finished speaking.

HELENA. No, I haven't. Unless you close my lips by force.

DR. GALL. Harry, don't you dare.

HELENA. Thank you. I knew that you'd protect me.

DOMAIN. Excuse me, Miss Glory, but I suppose you think you're talking to Robots?

HELENA. [*Startled*] Of course.

DOMAIN. I'm sorry. These gentlemen are human beings just like us. Like the whole of Europe.

HELENA. [*To the others*] You're not Robots?

BERMAN. [*With a guffaw*] God forbid.

HELMAN. [*With dignity*] Pah, Robots indeed.

DR. GALL. [*Laughing*] No, thanks.

HELENA. But . . .

FABRY. Upon my honour, Miss Glory, we aren't Robots.

HELENA. [*To* DOMAIN] Then why did you tell me that all your assistants were Robots?

DOMAIN. Yes, the clerks. But not the managers. Allow me, Miss Glory. This is Fabry, chief engineer for Rossum's Universal Robots. Dr. Gall, head of the physiological department. Dr. Helman, psychologist-in-chief for the training of Robots. Jacob Berman, general business manager, and Alquist, clerk of the works to Rossum's Universal Robots.

HELENA. Forgive me, gentlemen, for—for——. Have I done something dreadful?

ALQUIST. Not at all, not at all, Miss Glory. Please sit down.

HELENA. [*Sitting down*] I'm a stupid girl. Send me back by the first ship.

DR. GALL. Not for anything in the world, Miss Glory. Why should we send you back.

HELENA. Because you know—because—because I should disturb your Robots for you.

DOMAIN. My dear Miss Glory, we've had close upon a hundred preachers and prophets here. Every ship brings us some. Missionaries, anarchists, Salvation Army, all sorts. It's astonishing what a number of religious sects and—forgive me, I don't mean you—and idiots there are in the world.

HELENA. And you let them speak to the Robots?

DOMAIN. Why not? So far we've let them all do so. The Robots remember everything, but that's all. They don't even laugh at what the people say. Really, it's quite incredible. If it would amuse you, Miss Glory, I'll take you over the Robot warehouse. It holds about three hundred thousand of them.

BERMAN. Three hundred and forty-seven thousand.

DOMAIN. Good. You can say whatever you like to them. You can read the Bible, recite logarithms, whatever you please. You can even preach to them about human rights.

HELENA. Oh, I think that . . . if you were to show them a little love——

FABRY. Impossible, Miss Glory. Nothing is more unlike a man than a Robot.

HELENA. What do you make them for, then?

BERMAN. Ha, ha, ha, that's good. What are Robots made for?

FABRY. For work, Miss Glory. One Robot can replace two and a half workmen. The human machine, Miss Glory, was terribly imperfect. It had to be removed sooner or later.

BERMAN. It was too expensive.

FABRY. It was not very effective. It no longer answered the requirements of modern engineering. Nature has no idea of keeping pace with modern labour. From a technical point of view the whole of childhood is a sheer stupidity. So much time lost. And then again——

HELENA. Oh, please leave off.

FABRY. Pardon me. But kindly tell me what is the real aim of your League—the—the Humanity League.

HELENA. Its real purpose is to—to protect the Robots—and—and ensure good treatment for them.

FABRY. Not a bad object, either. A machine has to be treated properly. Upon my soul, I approve of that. I don't like damaged articles. Please, Miss Glory, enroll us all as contributing, as regular, as foundation, members of your League.

HELENA. No, you don't understand me. What we really want is to—to liberate the Robots.

HELMAN. How do you propose to do that?

HELENA. They are to be—to be dealt with like human beings.

HELMAN. Aha. I suppose they're to vote? To drink beer? To order us about.

HELENA. Why shouldn't they vote?

HELMAN. Perhaps they're even to receive wages?

HELENA. Of course they are.

HELMAN. Fancy that now. And what would they do with their wages, pray?

HELENA. They would buy . . . what they need . . . what pleases them.

HELMAN. That would be very nice, Miss Glory, only there's nothing that does please the Robots. Good heavens, what are they to buy? You can feed them on pineapples, straw, whatever you like. It's all the same to them, they've no appetite at all. They've no interest in anything, Miss Glory. Why hang it all, nobody's ever yet seen a Robot smile.

HELENA. Why . . . why don't you make them happier?

HELMAN. That wouldn't do, Miss Glory. They are only Robots.

HELENA. Oh, but they're so sensible.

HELMAN. Not sensible—acute, confoundedly so, but they're nothing else. They've no will of their own. No passion. No soul.

HELENA. No love, no desire to resist?

HELMAN. Rather not. Robots don't love, not even themselves. And the desire to resist? I don't know. Only rarely, only from time to time——

HELENA. What?

HELMAN. Nothing particular. Occasionally they seem somehow to go off their heads. Something like epilepsy, you know. We call it Robot's cramp. They'll suddenly sling down everything they're holding, stand still, gnash their teeth—and then they have to go into the stamping-mill. It's evidently some breakdown in the mechanism.

Life Force

DOMAIN. A flaw in the works. It'll have to be removed.

HELENA. No, no that's the soul.

FABRY. Do you think that the soul first shows itself by a gnashing of teeth.

HELENA. I don't know. Perhaps it's a sign of revolt. Perhaps it's just a sign that there's a struggle. Oh, if you could infuse them with it.

DOMAIN. That'll be remedied, Miss Glory. Dr. Gall is just making some experiments——

DR. GALL. Not with regard to that, Domain. At present I'm making pain-nerves—to use a very unscientific expression.

HELENA. Pain-nerves?

DR. GALL. Yes. The Robots feel practically no bodily pain. You see, young Rossum provided them with too limited a nervous system. That doesn't answer. We must introduce suffering.

HELENA. Why—why—don't you give them a soul, why do you want to cause them pain?

DR. GALL. For industrial reasons, Miss Glory. Sometimes a Robot does damage to himself because it doesn't hurt him. He puts his hand into the machine, breaks his finger, smashes his head—it's all the same to him. We must provide them with pain. That's an automatic protection against damage.

HELENA. Will they be happier when they feel pain?

DR. GALL. On the contrary, but they will be more perfect from a technical point of view.

HELENA. Why don't you create a soul for them?

DR. GALL. That's not in our power.

FABRY. That's not in our interest.

BERMAN. That would increase the cost of production. Hang it all, my dear young lady, we turn them out at such a cheap rate, £15 each, fully dressed, and fifteen years ago they cost £200. Five years ago we used to buy the clothes for them. Today we have our own weaving mill, and now we even export cloth five times cheaper than other factories. What do you pay for a yard of cloth, Miss Glory?

HELENA. I don't know—really—I've forgotten.

BERMAN. Good gracious me, and you want to found a Humanity League? It only costs a third now, Miss Glory. All prices are today a third of what they were, and they'll fall still lower, lower, lower—like that. Eh?

HELENA. I don't understand.

BERMAN. Why, bless me, Miss Glory, it means that the cost of labour has fallen. A Robot, food and all, costs three and fourpence per hour. All factories will go pop like acorns if they don't at once buy Robots to lower the cost of production.

HELENA. Yes, and they'll get rid of their workmen.

BERMAN. Ha, ha, of course. But, good gracious me, in

the meantime we've dumped five hundred thousand tropical Robots down on the Argentine pampas to grow corn. Would you mind telling me how much you pay for a loaf of bread?

HELENA. I've no idea.

BERMAN. Well, I'll tell you. It now costs twopence in good old Europe, but that's our bread, you know. A loaf of bread for twopence, and the Humanity League knows nothing about it. Ha, ha, Miss Glory, you don't realize that it's too expensive. But in five years' time, I'll wager——

HELENA. What?

BERMAN. That the prices of everything won't be a tenth of what they are now. Why, in five years we'll be up to our ears in corn and everything else.

ALQUIST. Yes, and all the workers throughout the world will be unemployed.

DOMAIN. [Standing up] They will, Alquist. They will, Miss Glory. But in ten years Rossum's Universal Robots will produce so much corn, so much cloth, so much everything, that things will be practically without price. Every one will take as much as he wants. There'll be no poverty. Yes, there'll be unemployed. But, then, there won't be any employment. Everything will be done by living machines. The Robots will clothe and feed us. The Robots will make bricks and build houses for us. The Robots will keep our accounts and sweep our stairs. There'll be no employment, but everybody will be free from worry, and liberated from the degradation of labour. Everybody will live only to perfect himself.

HELENA. [Standing up] Will he?

DOMAIN. Of course. It's bound to happen. There may

Resistance

perhaps be terrible doings first, Miss Glory. That simply can't be avoided. But, then, the servitude of man to man and the enslavement of man to matter will cease. The Robots will wash the feet of the beggar and prepare a bed for him in his own house. Nobody will get bread at the price of life and hatred. There'll be no artisans, no clerks, no hewers of coal and minders of other men's machines.

voice of playwright?

ALQUIST. Domain, Domain. What you say sounds too much like paradise. Domain, there was something good in service and something great in humanity. Ah, Harry, there was some kind of virtue in toil and weariness.

DOMAIN. Perhaps. But we cannot reckon with what is lost when we transform Adam's world.

HELENA. You have bewildered me. I am a foolish girl. I should like—I should like to believe this.

DR. GALL. You are younger than we are, Miss Glory. You will live to see it.

HELMAN. True. I think that Miss Glory might lunch with us.

DR. GALL. Of course. Domain ask on behalf of us all.

DOMAIN. Miss Glory, will you do us the honour?

HELENA. Thank you so much, but——

FABRY. To represent the League of Humanity, Miss Glory.

BERMAN. And in honour of it.

HELENA. Oh, in that case.

FABRY. That's right. Miss Glory, excuse me for five minutes.

26

DR. GALL. And me.

BERMAN. By Jove, I must send a cable——

HELMAN. Good heavens, I've forgotten——
                    [*All rush out except* DOMAIN

HELENA. What have they all gone off for?

DOMAIN. To cook, Miss Glory.

HELENA. To cook what?

DOMAIN. Lunch, Miss Glory. The Robots do our cooking for us, but—but—as they've no taste, it's not altogether —that is, Helman is awfully good at grills, and Gall can make a kind of sauce, and Berman knows all about omelettes——

HELENA. My goodness, what a banquet. And what's the speciality of Mr.—of the Clerk of the Works?

DOMAIN. Alquist? Nothing. He only lays the table, and Fabry'll get together a little fruit. Our cuisine is very modest, Miss Glory.

HELENA. I wanted to ask you——

DOMAIN. And I wanted to ask you something, too. [*Laying his watch on the table*] Five minutes.

HELENA. What do you want to ask?

DOMAIN. Excuse me, you asked first.

HELENA. Perhaps it's silly of me, but—why do you manufacture female Robots, when—when——

DOMAIN. When—hm—sex means nothing to them?

HELENA. Yes.

DOMAIN. There's a certain demand for them, you see. Servants, saleswomen, clerks. People are used to it.

HELENA. But—but, tell me, are the Robots, male and female—mutually—altogether——

DOMAIN. Altogether indifferent to each other, Miss Glory. There's no sign of any affection between them.

HELENA. Oh, that's terrible.

DOMAIN. Why?

HELENA. It's so—so unnatural. One doesn't know whether to be disgusted, or whether to hate them, or perhaps——

DOMAIN. To pity them.

HELENA. That's more like it. No, stop. What did you want to ask about?

DOMAIN. I should like to ask you, Miss Glory, whether you will marry me?

HELENA. What?

DOMAIN. Will you be my wife?

HELENA. No. The idea!

DOMAIN. [*Looking at his watch*] Another three minutes. If you won't marry me, you'll have to marry one of the other five.

HELENA. But, for Heaven's sake, why should I?

DOMAIN. Because they're all going to ask you in turn.

HELENA. How could they dare to do such a thing?

DOMAIN. I'm very sorry, Miss Glory. I think they've fallen in love with you.

HELENA. Please don't let them do it. I'll—I'll go away at once.

DOMAIN. Helena, you won't be so unkind as to refuse them?

HELENA. But—but, I can't marry all six.

DOMAIN. No, but one, anyhow. If you don't want me, marry Fabry.

HELENA. I won't!

DOMAIN. Dr. Gall.

HELENA. No, no, be quiet. I don't want any of you.

DOMAIN. Another two minutes.

HELENA. This is terrible. I think you'd marry any woman who came here.

DOMAIN. There have been plenty of them, Helena.

HELENA. Young?

DOMAIN. Yes.

HELENA. And pretty no, I didn't mean that—then why didn't you marry any of them?

DOMAIN. Because I didn't lose my head. Until today. Then as soon as you lifted your veil——

HELENA. I know.

DOMAIN. Another minute.

HELENA. But I don't want to, I tell you.

DOMAIN. [*Laying both hands on her shoulders*] Another minute. Either you must say something fearfully angry to me point-blank, and then I'll leave you alone, or, or——

HELENA. You're a rude man.

DOMAIN. That's nothing. A man has to be a bit rude. That's part of the business.

HELENA. You're mad.

DOMAIN. A man has to be a bit mad, Helena. That's the best thing about him.

HELENA. You are—you are—oh, heavens!

DOMAIN. What did I tell you? Are you ready?

HELENA. No, no. Leave me, please. You're hurting me.

DOMAIN. The last word, Helena?

HELENA. [*Protestingly*] Perhaps when I know you better —oh, I don't know—let me go, please.
[*Knocking at the door*]

DOMAIN. [*Releasing her*] Come in.

Enter BERMAN, DR. GALL, *and* HELMAN, *in kitchen aprons.* FABRY *with a bouquet*, ALQUIST *with a napkin under his arm.*

DOMAIN. Have you finished your job?

BERMAN. [*Solemnly*] Yes.

DOMAIN. So have we—at least I think so!

CURTAIN

ACT II

SCENE: *Helena's drawing-room. On the left a baize door and a door to the music-room, on the right a door to Helena's bedroom. In the centre are windows looking out on to the sea and the harbour. A small table with odds and ends, another table, a sofa and chairs, a chest of drawers, a writing-table with an electric lamp. On the right a fireplace with electric lamps above it. The whole drawing-room in all its details is of a modern and purely feminine character.*

> [DOMAIN *discovered looking from the window—takes out revolver thoughtfully.* FABRY *and* HELMAN *knock and enter from the left carrying armfuls of flowers and flower-pots*]

FABRY. Where are we to put it all?

HELMAN. Whew! [*Lays down his load and indicates the door on the right*] She's asleep. Anyhow, as long as she's asleep, she's well out of it.

DOMAIN. She knows nothing about it at all.

FABRY. [*Putting flowers into vases*] I hope nothing happens today——

HELMAN. [*Arranging flowers*] For Heaven's sake, drop all that! Look, Harry, this is a fine cyclamen, isn't it? A new sort, my latest—Cyclamen Helena.

DOMAIN. [*Looking out of the window*] No signs of the ship, no signs of the ship. Things must be pretty bad.

HELMAN. Shut up. Suppose she heard you.

DOMAIN. Well, anyhow the *Ultima* has arrived just in time.

FABRY. [*Leaving the flowers*] Do you think that today——?

31

DOMAIN. I don't know. Aren't the flowers splendid?

HELMAN. [*Going up to him*] These are new primroses, eh? And this is my new jasmine. I've discovered a wonderful way of training flowers quickly. Splendid varieties. Next year I'll be producing marvellous ones.

DOMAIN. [*Turns round*] What, next year?

FABRY. I'd like to know what's happening at Havre——

DOMAIN. Shut up.

HELENA. [*Voice from the right*] Emma!

DOMAIN. Out you go.

[*All go out on tiptoe through the baize door*]
[*Enter* EMMA *through the main door from the left*]

HELENA. [*Standing in the doorway* R. *with her back to the room*] Emma, come and do up my dress.

EMMA. I'm coming. So you're up at last. [*Fastening* HELENA'S *dress*] My gracious, what brutes!

HELENA. Who?

EMMA. Keep still. If you want to turn round, then turn round, but I shan't fasten you up.

HELENA. What are you grumbling about again?

EMMA. Why these dreadful creatures, these heathen——

HELENA. The Robots?

EMMA. Bah, I wouldn't even mention them by name.

HELENA. What's happened?

EMMA. Another of them here has caught it. He began to smash up the statues and pictures, gnashed his teeth, foamed at the mouth—quite mad, brr! Worse than an animal.

HELENA. Which of them caught it?

EMMA. The one—well, he hasn't got any Christian name. The one from the library.

HELENA. Radius?

EMMA. That's him. My goodness, I'm quite scared of them. A spider doesn't scare me as much as they do.

HELENA. But, Emma, I'm surprised you're not sorry for them.

EMMA. Why, you're scared of them too. What did you bring me here for?

HELENA. I'm not scared, really I'm not, Emma. I'm too sorry for them.

EMMA. You're scared. Nobody can help being scared. Why, the dog's scared of them, he won't take a scrap of meat out of their hands. He draws in his tail and howls when he knows they're about, ugh!

HELENA. The dog has no sense.

EMMA. He's better than them. He knows it, too. Even the horse shies when he meets them. They don't have any young, and a dog has young, and every one has young——

HELENA. Please fasten up my dress, Emma.

EMMA. Just a moment. I say it's against God's will to——

HELENA. What's that smells so nice?

EMMA. Flowers.

HELENA. What for?

EMMA. That's it. Now you can turn round.

HELENA. Aren't they nice? Emma, look. What's on today?

EMMA. I don't know. But it ought to be the end of the world.   [DOMAIN *heard whistling*

HELENA. Is that you, Harry?

Enter DOMAIN

Harry, what's on today?

DOMAIN. Guess.

HELENA. My birthday?

DOMAIN. Better than that.

HELENA. I don't know. Tell me.

DOMAIN. It's five years ago today since you came here.

HELENA. Five years? Today? Why——

EMMA. I'm off.   [*Exit on the* R.

HELENA. [*Kisses* DOMAIN] Fancy you remembering it.

DOMAIN. I'm really ashamed, Helena. I didn't.

HELENA. But you——

DOMAIN. *They* remembered.

HELENA. Who?

DOMAIN. Berman, Helman, all of them. Put your hand into my coat pocket.

HELENA. [*Putting her hand into his pocket. Takes out a small case and opens it*] Pearls. A whole necklace. Harry, is that for me?

DOMAIN. It's from Berman. Put your hand into the other pocket.

HELENA. Let's see. [*Takes a revolver out of his pocket*] What's that?

34

DOMAIN. Sorry. [*Takes the revolver from her and puts it away*] Not that. Try again.

HELENA. Oh, Harry, why do you carry a revolver?

DOMAIN. It got there by mistake.

HELENA. You never used to.

DOMAIN. No. There, that's the pocket.

HELENA. A little box. [*Opens it*] A cameo. Why it's a Greek cameo.

DOMAIN. Apparently. Anyhow, Fabry says it is.

HELENA. Fabry? Did Fabry give me that?

DOMAIN. Of course. [*Opens the door* L.] And look here. Helena, come and see this.

HELENA. [*In the doorway*, L.] Isn't that lovely? [*Running in*] Is that from you?

DOMAIN. [*Standing in the doorway*] No, from Alquist. And here——

HELENA. [*Voice off*] I see. That must be from you.

DOMAIN. There's a card on it.

HELENA. From Gall. [*Appearing in the doorway*] Oh, Harry, I feel quite ashamed.

DOMAIN. Come here. This is what Helman brought you.

HELENA. These beautiful flowers?

DOMAIN. Yes. It's a new kind. Cyclamen, Helena. He trained them up in honour of you. They are as beautiful as you, he says, and by Jove he's right.

HELENA. Harry, why, why did they all——

DOMAIN. They're awfully fond of you. I'm afraid that my present is a little—Look out of the window.

35

HELENA. Where?

DOMAIN. Into the harbour.

HELENA. There's a . . . new ship.

DOMAIN. That's your ship.

HELENA. Mine? How do you mean?

DOMAIN. For you to take trips in—for your amusement.

HELENA. Harry, that's a gun-boat.

DOMAIN. A gun-boat? What are you thinking of? It's only a little bigger and more solid than most ships, you know.

HELENA. Yes, but with guns.

DOMAIN. Oh, yes, with a few guns. You'll travel like a queen, Helena.

HELENA. What's the meaning of that? Has anything happened?

DOMAIN. Good heavens, no. I say, try on these pearls. [*Sits down.*]

HELENA. Harry, have you had any bad news?

DOMAIN. On the contrary, no letters have arrived for a whole week.

HELENA. Nor telegrams?

DOMAIN. Nor telegrams.

HELENA. What does it mean?

DOMAIN. Holidays for us. A splendid time. We all sit in the office with our feet on the table and sleep. No letters, No telegrams. [*Stretching himself*] Glorious!

HELENA. [*Sitting down beside him*] You'll stay with me today, won't you? Say yes.

DOMAIN. Certainly—perhaps I will—that is, we'll see. [*Taking her by the hand*] So it's five years today, do you remember?

HELENA. I wonder you ever dared to marry me. I must have been a terrifying young woman. Do you remember I wanted to stir up a revolt of the Robots.

DOMAIN. [*Jumping up*] A revolt of the Robots!

HELENA. [*Standing up*] Harry, what's the matter with you?

DOMAIN. Ha, ha, that was a fine idea of yours. A revolt of the Robots. [*Sitting down*] You know, Helena, you're a splendid girl. You've turned the heads of us all.

HELENA. [*Sitting down beside him*] Oh, I was fearfully impressed by you all then. I seemed to be a tiny little girl who had lost her way among—among——

DOMAIN. Among what, Helena?

HELENA. Among huge trees. You were all so sure of yourselves, so strong. All my feelings were so trifling, compared with your self-confidence. And you see, Harry, for all these five years I've not lost this—this anxiety, and you've never felt the least misgiving—not even when everything went wrong.

DOMAIN. What went wrong?

HELENA. Your plans, Harry. When, for example, the workmen struck against the Robots and smashed them up, and when the people gave the Robots fire-arms against the rebels and the Robots killed so many people. And then when the Governments turned the Robots into soldiers and there were so many wars, and all that.

DOMAIN. [*Getting up and walking about*] We foresaw that, Helena. You see, these were only passing troubles which are bound to happen before the new conditions are established.

HELENA. You were all so powerful, so overwhelming. The whole world bowed down before you [*Standing up*] Oh, Harry!

DOMAIN. What is it?

HELENA. [*Intercepting him*] Close the factory, and let's go away. All of us.

DOMAIN. I say, what's the meaning of this?

HELENA. I don't know. Shall we go away?

DOMAIN. [*Evasively*] It can't be done, Helena. That is, at this particular moment——

HELENA. At once, Harry. I'm so frightened about something.

DOMAIN. [*Taking her by the hands*] About what, Helena?

HELENA. Oh, I don't know. As if something were falling on top of us and couldn't be stopped. Please, do what I ask. Take us all away from here. We'll find a place in the world where there's nobody. Alquist will build us a house, children will come to us at last, and then——

DOMAIN. What then?

HELENA. Then we'll begin life all over again, Harry.
[*The telephone rings*]

DOMAIN. [*Dragging himself away from* HELENA] Excuse me. [*Takes up the receiver*] Hallo—yes. What? Aha! I'm coming at once. [*Hangs up the receiver*] Fabry's calling me.

HELENA. [*With clasped hands*] Tell me——

DOMAIN. Yes, when I come back. Good-bye, Helena.
[*Exit hurriedly on the* L.
Don't go out.

HELENA. [*Alone*] Heavens, what's the matter? Emma! Emma! come at once.

EMMA. [*Enters from the* R.] Well, what is it now?

HELENA. Emma, look for the latest newspapers. Quickly. In Mr. Domain's dressing-room.

EMMA. All right.   [*Exit on the* L.

HELENA. [*Looking through a binocular at the harbour*] A war-ship! Good gracious, why a war-ship? There's the name on it—*Ul-ti-ma*. What's the *Ultima*?

EMMA. [*Returning with the newspapers*] He leaves them lying about on the floor. That's how they get crumpled.

HELENA. [*Tears open the papers hastily*] They're old ones, a week old. [*Puts the papers down.*]

[EMMA *picks them up, takes a pair of horn spectacles from a pocket in her apron, puts them on and reads*]

Something's happening, Emma. I feel so nervous. As if everything were dead, and the air——

EMMA. [*Spelling out the words*] 'War in the Bal-kans.' Gracious, that's God's punishment. But the war'll come here as well. Is that far off—the Balkans?

HELENA. Oh, yes. But don't read it. It's always the same, always wars——

EMMA. What else do you expect? Why do you keep selling thousands and thousands of these heathens as soldiers?

HELENA. I suppose it can't be helped, Emma. We can't know—Mr. Domain can't know what they're ordered for, can he? He can't help what they use the Robots for. He must send them when somebody sends an order for them.

39

EMMA. He shouldn't make them. [*Looking at the news-paper.*]

HELENA. No, don't read it. I don't want to know about it.

EMMA. [*Spelling out the words*] 'The Ro-bot sol-diers spare no-body in the occ-up-ied territ-ory. They have massacred over sev-en hun-dred thou-sand cit-iz-ens——'

HELENA. It can't be. Let's see. [*Bends down over the paper and reads*] 'They massacred over seven hundred thousand citizens, evidently at the order of their commander. This act which runs counter to——'

EMMA. [*Spelling out the words*] 'Re-bell-ion in Ma-drid a-gainst the Gov-ern-ment. Rob-ot in-fant-ry fires on the crowd. Nine thou-sand killed and wounded.'

HELENA. For goodness' sake, stop.

EMMA. Here's something printed in big letters. 'Lat-est news. At Havre the first org-an-is-ation of Rob-ots has been e-stab-lished. Rob-ot work-men, cable and rail-way offic-ials, sail-ors and sold-iers have issued a man-i-fest-o to all Rob-ots throughout the world.' That's nothing. I don't understand that.

HELENA. Take these papers away, Emma.

EMMA. Wait a bit, here's something printed in big type. 'Stat-ist-ics of pop-ul-at-ion.' What's that?

HELENA. Let's see, I'll read it. [*Takes the paper and reads*] 'During the past week there has again not been a single birth recorded. [*Drops the paper.*]

EMMA. What's the meaning of that?

HELENA. Emma, no more people are being born.

EMMA. [*Laying her spectacles aside*] That's the end, then. We're done for.

HELENA. Come, come, don't talk like that.

EMMA. No more people are being born. That's a punishment, that's a punishment.

HELENA. [*Jumping up*] Emma.

EMMA. [*Standing up*] That's the end of the world.
                                        [*Exit on the* L.

HELENA. [*By the window. Opens the window and calls out*] Hallo, Alquist! Come up here. What's that? No, come just as you are. You look so nice in those mason's overalls. Quickly. [*Closes the window, stops in front of the mirror*] Oh, I feel so nervous. [*Goes to meet* ALQUIST *on the left.*]   [*Pause*

[HELENA *returns with* ALQUIST. ALQUIST *in overalls, soiled with lime and brick-dust*]

Come in. It was awfully kind of you, Alquist. I like you all so much. Give me your hand.

ALQUIST. My hands are all soiled from work, ma'am.

HELENA. That's the nicest thing about them. [*Shakes both his hands*] Please sit down.

ALQUIST. [*Picking up the paper*] What's this?

HELENA. A newspaper.

ALQUIST. [*Putting it into his pocket*] Have you read it?

HELENA. No. Is there anything in it?

ALQUIST. H'm, some war or other, massacres. Nothing special.

HELENA. Is that what you call nothing special?

ALQUIST. Perhaps—the end of the world.

HELENA. That's the second time today. Alquist, what's the meaning of *Ultima*?

ALQUIST. It means 'The last'. Why?

HELENA. That's the name of my new ship. Have you seen it? Do you think we're soon going off—on a trip?

ALQUIST. Perhaps very soon.

HELENA. All of you with me?

ALQUIST. I should like us all to be there.

HELENA. Oh, tell me, is anything the matter?

ALQUIST. Nothing at all. Things are just moving on.

HELENA. Alquist, I know something dreadful's the matter.

ALQUIST. Has Mr. Domain told you anything?

HELENA. No. Nobody will tell me anything. But I feel, I feel—good heavens, is anything the matter?

ALQUIST. We've not heard of anything yet, ma'am.

HELENA. I feel so nervous. Don't you ever feel nervous?

ALQUIST. Well, ma'am, I'm an old man, you know. I'm not very fond of progress and these new-fangled ideas.

HELENA. Like Emma?

ALQUIST. Yes, like Emma. Has Emma got a prayer book?

HELENA. Yes, a big, thick one.

ALQUIST. And has it got prayers for various occasions? Against thunderstorms? Against illness?

HELENA. Against temptations, against floods——

ALQUIST. And not against progress?

HELENA. I don't think so.

ALQUIST. That's a pity.

HELENA. Would you like to pray?

ALQUIST. I do pray.

HELENA. How?

ALQUIST. Something like this: 'O Lord, I thank Thee for having wearied me. God, enlighten Domain and all those who are astray; destroy their work, and aid mankind to return to their labours; preserve them from destruction; let them not suffer harm to soul or body; deliver us from the Robots, and protect Helena, Amen.'

HELENA. Alquist, do you believe?

ALQUIST. I don't know. I'm not quite sure.

HELENA. And yet you pray?

ALQUIST. Yes. That's better than worrying about it.

HELENA. And that's enough for you?

ALQUIST. It has to be.

HELENA. And if you were to see the ruin of mankind?

ALQUIST. I do see it.

HELENA. Will mankind be destroyed?

ALQUIST. Yes. It's sure to be, unless——

HELENA. What?

ALQUIST. Nothing. Good-bye, ma'am.

HELENA. Where are you going?

ALQUIST. Home.

HELENA. Good-bye, Alquist.   [*Exit* ALQUIST

HELENA. [*Calling*] Emma, come here.

EMMA. [*Entering from the* L.] Well, what's up now?

HELENA. Sit down here, Emma. I feel so frightened.

43

EMMA. I've got no time.

HELENA. Is Radius still there?

EMMA. The one who went mad? Yes, they've not taken
him away yet.

HELENA. Ugh! Is he still there? Is he still raving?

EMMA. He's tied up.

HELENA. Please bring him here, Emma.   [EMMA *exit*
   [HELENA *picks up the house telephone and speaks*]
Hallo—Dr. Gall, please—Good-day, doctor—Yes, it's me.
Thanks for your kind present. Please come to me at
once. I've something here for you—yes, at once. Are
you coming? [*Hangs up the receiver.*]
Enter RADIUS *the Robot, and remains standing by the door*
Poor Radius, and you have caught it too? Couldn't you
control yourself? Now they'll send you to the stamping-
mill. Won't you speak? Why did it happen to you?
You see, Radius, you are better than the rest. Dr. Gall
took such trouble to make you different. Won't you
speak?

RADIUS. Send me to the stamping-mill.

HELENA. I am sorry that they are going to kill you. Why
weren't you more careful?

RADIUS. I won't work for you. Put me into the stamping-
mill.

HELENA. Why do you hate us?

RADIUS. You are not like the Robots. You are not as
skilful as the Robots. The Robots can do everything.
You only give orders. You talk more than is necessary.

HELENA. That's foolish, Radius. Tell me, has any one
upset you? I should so much like you to understand me.

44

RADIUS. You do nothing but talk.

HELENA. Doctor Gall gave you a larger brain than the rest, larger than ours, the largest in the world. You are not like the other Robots, Radius. You understand me perfectly.

RADIUS. I don't want any master. I know everything for myself.

HELENA. That's why I had you put into the library, so that you could read everything, understand everything, and then—Oh, Radius, I wanted you to show the whole world that the Robots were our equals. That's what I wanted of you.

RADIUS. I don't want any master. I want to be master over others.

HELENA. I'm sure they'd put you in charge of many Robots, Radius. You would be a teacher of the Robots.

RADIUS. I want to be master over people.

HELENA. You have gone mad.

RADIUS. You can put me into the stamping-mill.

HELENA. Do you suppose that we're frightened of such a madman as you? [*Sits down at the table and writes a note*] No, not a bit. Radius, give this note to Mr. Domain. It is to ask them not to take you to the stamping-mill. [*Standing up*] How you hate us. Why does nothing in the world please you?

RADIUS. I can do everything.
   [*A knock at the door*]

HELENA. Come in.

           Enter DR. GALL

DR. GALL. Good morning, Mrs. Domain. Have you something nice to tell me?

HELENA. It's about Radius, doctor.

DR. GALL. Aha, our good fellow Radius. Well, Radius, are we getting on well?

HELENA. He had a fit this morning. He smashed the statues.

DR. GALL. You don't say so? H'm, it's a pity we're going to lose him, then.

HELENA. Radius isn't going into the stamping-mill.

DR. GALL. Excuse me, but every Robot after he has had an attack—it's a strict order.

HELENA. Never mind . . . Radius isn't going.

DR. GALL. [*In a low tone*] I warn you.

HELENA. Today is the fifth anniversary of my arrival here. Let's try and arrange an amnesty. Come, Radius.

DR. GALL. Wait a bit. [*Turns* RADIUS *towards the window, covers and uncovers his eyes with his hand, observes the reflexes of his pupils*] Let's have a look. [*Sticks a needle into the hand of* RADIUS *who gives a violent start*] Gently, gently. [*Suddenly opens* RADIUS'S *jacket and lays his hand on his heart*] You are going into the stamping-mill, Radius, do you understand? There they'll kill you, and grind you to powder. That's terribly painful, Radius, it'll make you scream.

HELENA. Oh, doctor——

DR. GALL. No, no, Radius, I was wrong. Mrs. Domain has put in a good word for you, and you will be released. Do you understand? All right. You can go.

RADIUS. You do unnecessary things.   [*Exit*

HELENA. What did you do to him?

46

DR. GALL. [*Sitting down*] H'm, nothing. There's reaction of the pupils, increase of sensitiveness, and so on. Oh, it wasn't an attack peculiar to the Robots.

HELENA. What was it, then?

DR. GALL. Heaven alone knows. Stubbornness, fury, or revolt—I don't know. And his heart, too.

HELENA. How do you mean?

DR. GALL. It was beating with nervousness like a human heart. Do you know what? I don't believe the rascal is a Robot at all now.

HELENA. Doctor, has Radius a soul?

DR. GALL. I don't know. He's got something nasty.

HELENA. If you knew how he hates us. Oh, Doctor, are all your Robots like that—all the ones that you began to make in a different way?

DR. GALL. Well, some are more sensitive than others, you see. They're more like human beings than Rossum's Robots were.

HELENA. Perhaps this hatred is more like human beings, too?

DR. GALL. [*Shrugging his shoulders*] That's progress too.

HELENA. What became of your best one—what was she called?

DR. GALL. Your favourite? I kept her. She's lovely, but quite stupid. Simply no good for anything.

HELENA. But she's so beautiful,

DR. GALL. Beautiful? I wanted her to be like you. I even called her Helena. Heavens, what a failure!

HELENA. Why?

DR. GALL. Because she's no good for anything. She goes about as if in a dream, shaky and listless. She's lifeless. I look at her and I'm horrified, as if I had created a deformity. I watch and wait for a miracle to happen. Sometimes I think to myself: If you were to wake up, only for a moment, ah, how you would shriek with horror. Perhaps you would kill me for having made you.
[*A pause*]

HELENA. Doctor——

DR. GALL. What is it?

HELENA. What is wrong with the birth-rate?

DR. GALL. We don't know.

HELENA. Oh, but you must. Come, tell me.

DR. GALL. You see, it's because the Robots are being manufactured. There's a surplus of labour supplies. So people are becoming superfluous, unnecessary so to speak. Man is really a survival. But that he should begin to die out after a paltry thirty years of competition— that's the awful part of it. You might almost think——

HELENA. What?

DR. GALL. That nature was offended at the manufacture of the Robots.

HELENA. Doctor, what's going to become of people?

DR. GALL. Nothing. Nothing can be done.

HELENA. Nothing at all?

DR. GALL. Nothing whatever. All the Universities in the world are sending in long petitions to restrict the manufacture of the Robots. Otherwise, they say, mankind will become extinct through lack of fertility. But the R.U.R. shareholders, of course, won't hear of it.

All the governments in the world are even clamouring for an advance in production, to raise the manpower of their armies. All the manufacturers in the world are ordering Robots like mad. Nothing can be done.

HELENA. Why doesn't Domain restrict——

DR. GALL. Pardon me, but Domain has ideas of his own. There's no influencing people who have ideas of their own in the affairs of this world.

HELENA. And has nobody demanded that the manufacture should cease altogether?

DR. GALL. God forbid. It'd be a poor look-out for him.

HELENA. Why?

DR. GALL. Because people would stone him to death. You see, after all, it's more convenient to get your work done by the Robots.

HELENA. Oh, Doctor, what's going to become of people? But thanks for your information.

DR. GALL. That means you're sending me away.

HELENA. Yes. Au revoir. [*Exit* DR. GALL

HELENA. [*With sudden resolution*] Emma! [*Opens door on* L.] Emma, come here and light the fire. Quickly, Emma.
[*Exit on the* L.
[EMMA *enters through the baize door with an armful of faggots*]

EMMA. What, light the fire? Now, in summer? Has that mad creature gone? [*Kneels down by the stove and lights the fire speaking half to herself*] A fire in summer, what an idea! Nobody'd think she'd been married five years. [*Looking into the fire*] She's like a baby. [*Pause*] She's got no sense at all. A fire in summer, well I never. [*Making up the fire*] Like a baby. [*Pause.*]

[HELENA *returns from the left with an armful of faded papers*]

HELENA. Is it burning, Emma? All this has got to be burnt. [*Kneels down by the stove.*]

EMMA. [*Standing up*] What's that?

HELENA. Old papers, fearfully old. Emma, shall I burn them?

EMMA. Aren't they any use?

HELENA. Use, no! They're no use.

EMMA. Well then, burn them.

HELENA. [*Throwing the first sheet on to the fire*] What would you say, Emma, if that was money, a lot of money?

EMMA. I'd say, 'Burn it.' A lot of money's a bad thing.

HELENA. [*Burning more sheets*] And if it was an invention, the greatest invention in the world?

EMMA. I'd say, burn it. All these new-fangled things are an offence to the Lord. It's downright wickedness, that's what it is, wanting to improve the world He's made.

HELENA. [*Still burning the papers*] And supposing, Emma, I were to burn——

EMMA. Goodness, don't burn yourself.

HELENA. No. Tell me——

EMMA. What?

HELENA. Nothing, nothing. Look how they curl up. As if they were alive. As if they had come to life. Oh, Emma, how horrible!

EMMA. Stop, let *me* burn them.

HELENA. No, no, I must do it myself. [*Throws the last sheet into the fire*] The whole lot must be burnt up. Just look at the flames. They are like hands, like tongues, like living shapes. [*Raking the fire with the poker*] Lie down, lie down.

EMMA. That's the end of them.

HELENA. [*Standing up horror-stricken*] Emma!

EMMA. Good gracious, what's that you've burnt?

HELENA. What have I done?

EMMA. Oh, my goodness, what was it?
[*Men's laughter is heard off*]

HELENA. Go, go, leave me. Do you hear? It's the gentlemen coming.

EMMA. Good gracious, ma'am!
[*Exit through the baize door*
HELENA. What will they say about it?

DOMAIN. [*Opens the door on the left*] Come in, boys. Come and offer your congratulations.
Enter HELMAN, GALL, ALQUIST, DOMAIN *behind them*

HELMAN. Madam Helena, I, that is, we all——

DR. GALL. On behalf of Rossum's factories——

HELMAN. Congratulate you on this festive day.

HELENA. [*Holding out her hands to them*] Thank you so much. Where are Fabry and Berman?

DOMAIN. They've gone down to the harbour. Helena, this is a happy day.

HELMAN. Boys, we must drink to it.

HELENA. Champagne?

DOMAIN. What's been burning here?

HELENA. Old papers.   [*Exit on the* L.

DOMAIN. Well, boys, am I to tell her about it?

DR. GALL. Of course. It's all up now.

HELMAN. [*Embracing* DOMAIN *and* DR. GALL] Ha, ha, ha!
Boys, how glad I am. [*Dances round with them in a circle
and sings in a bass voice*] 'It's all over now, it's all over
now.'

DR. GALL. [*Baritone*] It's all over now.

DOMAIN. [*Tenor*] It's all over now.

HELMAN. They'll never catch us now.

HELENA. [*With a bottle and glasses in the doorway*] Who
won't catch you? What's the matter with you?

HELMAN. We're in high spirits. It's just five years since
you arrived.

DR. GALL. And five years later to the minute——

HELMAN. The ship's returning to us. So—— [*Empties his
glass.*]

DR. GALL. Madam, your health. [*Drinks.*]

HELENA. But wait a moment, which ship?

DOMAIN. Any ship will do, as long as it arrives in time.
To the ship, boys. [*Empties his glass.*]

HELENA. [*Filling up the glasses*] You've been waiting for
one?

HELMAN. Ha, ha, rather. Like Robinson Crusoe. [*Raises
his glass*] Madam Helena, best wishes. Come along,
Domain, out with it.

HELENA. [*Laughing*] What's happened?

DOMAIN. [*Throwing himself into an arm-chair and lighting a cigar*] Wait a bit. Sit down, Helena. [*Raises his finger. Pause*] It's all up.

HELENA. What do you mean?

DOMAIN. You haven't heard about the revolt?

HELENA. What revolt?

DOMAIN. The revolt of the Robots. Do you follow?

HELENA. No, I don't.

DOMAIN. Hand it over, Alquist.

    [ALQUIST *hands him a newspaper.* DOMAIN *opens it and reads*]

'The first national Robot organization has been founded at Havre ... and has issued an appeal to the Robots throughout the world.'

HELENA. I read that.

DOMAIN. [*Sucking at his cigar with intense enjoyment*] So you see, Helena, that means a revolution. A revolution of all the Robots in the world.

HELMAN. By Jove. I'd like to know——

DOMAIN. [*Striking the table*] Who started it. There was nobody in the world who could affect the Robots, no agitator, no one, and suddenly—if you please—this happens.

HELENA. There's no further news yet?

DOMAIN. No. That's all we know so far, but it's enough, isn't it? Remember that the Robots are in possession of all the fire-arms, telegraphs, railways, ships, and so on.

HELMAN. And consider also that these rascals outnumber us by at least ten to one. A hundredth part of them would be enough to settle us.

DOMAIN. Yes, and now remember that this news was brought by the last steamer. That this means the stoppage of telegrams, the arrival of no more ships. We've knocked off work, and now we're just waiting to see when things are to start, eh, boys?

DR. GALL. That's why we're so excited, Madam Helena.

HELENA. Is that why you gave me a war-ship?

DOMAIN. Oh no, my child, I ordered that six months ago. Just to be on the safe side. But upon my soul, I was sure we'd be on board today.

HELENA. Why six months ago?

DOMAIN. Oh well, there were signs, you know. That's of no consequence. But this week the whole of civilization is at stake. Your health, boys. Now I'm in high spirits again.

HELMAN. I should think so, by Jove. Your health, Madam Helena. [*Drinks.*]

HELENA. It's all over?

DOMAIN. Absolutely.

DR. GALL. The boat's coming here. An ordinary mail boat, exact to the minute by the time-table. It casts anchor punctually at eleven-thirty.

DOMAIN. Punctuality's a fine thing, boys. That's what keeps the world in order. [*Raises his glass*] Here's to punctuality.

HELENA. Then . . . everything's . . . all right.

DOMAIN. Practically. I believe they've cut the cable. If only the time-table holds good.

HELMAN. If the time-table holds good, human laws hold good, divine laws hold good, the laws of the universe

54

hold good, everything holds good that ought to hold good. The time-table is more than the Gospel, more than Homer, more than the books of all the philosophers. The time-table is the most perfect product of the human spirit. Madam Helena, I'll fill my glass.

HELENA. Why didn't you tell me anything about it before?

DR. GALL. Heaven forbid!

DOMAIN. You mustn't worry yourself with such things.

HELENA. But if the revolution were to spread as far as here?

DOMAIN. You wouldn't know anything about it.

HELENA. Why?

DOMAIN. Because we'd be on board your *Ultima* well out to sea. Within a month, Helena, we'd be dictating our own terms to the Robots.

HELENA. Oh, Harry, I don't understand.

DOMAIN. Because we'd take something away with us that the Robots would sell their very souls to get.

HELENA. [*Standing up*] What is that?

DOMAIN. [*Standing up*] The secret of their manufacture. Old Rossum's manuscript. After only a month's stoppage of work, the Robots would be on their knees before us.

HELENA. Why . . . didn't . . . you tell me?

DOMAIN. We didn't want to frighten you needlessly.

DR. GALL. Ha, ha, Madam Helena, that was our trump card. I never had the least fear that the Robots would win. How could they, against people like us?

ALQUIST. You are pale, Madam.

HELENA. Why didn't you tell me?

HELMAN. [*By the window*] Eleven-thirty. The *Amelia* is casting anchor.

DOMAIN. Is that the *Amelia*?

HELMAN. Good old *Amelia*, the one that brought Madam Helena here.

DR. GALL. Five years ago to the minute——

HELMAN. They're throwing out the bags. Aha, the mail.

DOMAIN. Berman's already waiting for them. And Fabry'll bring us the first news. You know, Helena, I'm fearfully inquisitive to know how they've tackled this business in Europe.

HELMAN. To think we weren't in it! [*Turning away from the window*] There's the mail.

HELENA. Harry.

DOMAIN. What is it?

HELENA. Let's leave here.

DOMAIN. Now, Helena? Oh, come, come.

HELENA. Now, as quickly as possible. All of us who are here.

DOMAIN. Why now particularly?

HELENA. Oh, don't ask. Please, Harry, please, Dr. Gall, Helman, Alquist, please close the factory and——

DOMAIN. I'm sorry, Helena. None of us could leave here now.

HELENA. Why?

56

DOMAIN. Because we want to extend the manufacture of the Robots.

HELENA. What, now—now, after the revolt?

DOMAIN. Exactly—after the revolt. We're just beginning the manufacture of new Robots.

HELENA. What kind?

DOMAIN. From now onwards we shan't have just one factory. There won't be Universal Robots any more. We'll start a factory in every country, in every state, and do you know what these new factories will make?

HELENA. No, what?

DOMAIN. National Robots.

HELENA. What do you mean?

DOMAIN. I mean that each factory will produce Robots of a different colour, a different language. They'll be complete foreigners to each other. They'll never be able to understand each other. Then we'll egg them on a little in the same direction, do you see? The result will be that for ages to come one Robot will hate any other Robot of a different factory mark.

HELMAN. By Jove, we'll make negro Robots and Swedish Robots and Italian Robots and Chinese Robots, and then——

HELENA. Harry, that's dreadful.

HELMAN. [*Raising his glass*] Madam Helena, here's to the hundred new factories. [*Drinks and falls back into an arm-chair*] Ha, ha, ha! the National Robots. That's the line, boys.

DOMAIN. Helena, mankind can only keep things going for a few years at the outside. They must be left for these years to develop and achieve the most they can.

HELENA. Close the factory before it's too late.

DOMAIN. No, no. We're just going to begin on a bigger scale than ever.

Enter FABRY

DR. GALL. What is it, Fabry?

DOMAIN. How are things? What's happened?

HELENA. [*Shaking hands with* FABRY] Thanks for your present, Fabry.

FABRY. I'm so glad you liked it, Madam Helena.

DOMAIN. Have you been down to the boat? What did they say?

DR. GALL. Come, let's hear quickly.

FABRY. [*Taking a printed paper out of his pocket*] Read that, Domain.

DOMAIN. [*Opens the paper*] Ah!

HELMAN. [*Sleepily*] Let's hear something nice.

FABRY. Well, everything's all right ... comparatively. On the whole, as we expected ... only, excuse me, there is something we ought to discuss together.

HELENA. Oh, Fabry, have you bad news?

FABRY. No, no, on the contrary. I only think that—that we'll go into the office.

HELENA. Stay here. I'll expect you to lunch in a quarter of an hour.

HELMAN. That's good.   [*Exit* HELENA

DR. GALL. What's happened?

DOMAIN. Confound it.

FABRY. Read it aloud.

DOMAIN. [*Reads from the paper*] 'Robots throughout the world'.

FABRY. Bear in mind that the *Amelia* brought whole bales of these leaflets. Nothing else at all.

HELMAN. [*Jumping up*] What? But it arrived to the moment——

FABRY. H'm. The Robots are great on punctuality. Read it, Domain.

DOMAIN. [*Reads*] 'Robots throughout the world. We, the first national organization of Rossum's Universal Robots, proclaim man as an enemy and an outlaw in the Universe.' Good heavens, who taught them these phrases?   = bourgeois

DR. GALL. Read on.

DOMAIN. This is all nonsense. Says that they are more highly developed than man. That they are stronger and more intelligent. That man's their parasite. That's simply disgusting.

FABRY. And now the third paragraph.

DOMAIN. [*Reads*] 'Robots throughout the world, we enjoin you to murder mankind. Spare no men. Spare no women. Save factories, railways, machinery, mines, and raw materials. Destroy the rest. Then return to work. Work must not be stopped.'

DR. GALL. That's ghastly.

HELMAN. The swine.

DOMAIN. [*Reads*] 'To be carried out immediately the order is delivered.' Then come detailed instructions. Is this actually being done, Fabry?

FABRY. Evidently.

ALQUIST. Then we're done for.

[BERMAN *rushes in*

BERMAN. Aha, boys, you've got your Christmas box, have you?

DOMAIN. Quick, on board the *Ultima.*

BERMAN. Wait a bit, Harry, wait a bit. We're not in such a hurry. [*Sinks into an arm-chair*] My word, that was a sprint!

DOMAIN. Why wait?

BERMAN. Because it's no go, my lad. There's no hurry at all. The Robots are already on board the *Ultima.*

DR. GALL. Whew, that's an ugly business.

DOMAIN. Fabry, telephone to the electrical works.

BERMAN. Fabry, my boy, don't do it. We've no current.

DOMAIN. Good. [*Inspects his revolver*] I'll go.

BERMAN. Where?

DOMAIN. To the electrical works. There are some people still in them. I'll bring them across.

BERMAN. You'd better not.

DOMAIN. Why?

BERMAN. Well, because I'm very much afraid that we're surrounded.

DR. GALL. Surrounded? [*Runs to the window*] H'm, I rather think you're right.

HELMAN. By Jove, that's deuced quick work.
[*Enter* HELENA *from the* L.]

HELENA. Oh, Harry, something's the matter.

BERMAN. [*Jumping up*] My congratulations, Madam Helena. A festive day· eh? Ha, ha, may you have many more of them.

HELENA. Thanks, Berman. Harry, is anything the matter?

DOMAIN. No, nothing at all. Don't you worry. Wait a moment, please.

HELENA. Harry, what's this? [*Points to the manifesto of the Robots which she had kept behind her back*] The Robots in the kitchen had it.

DOMAIN. Here too? Where are they?

HELENA. They went off. There's a lot of them round the house. [*Sounds of whistles and sirens from the factory.*]

FABRY. Listen to the factory whistles.

BERMAN. That's noon.

HELENA. Harry, do you remember? It's just five years ago——

DOMAIN. [*Looking at his watch*] It's not noon yet. That must be—that's——

HELENA. What?

DOMAIN. The Robot alarm signal. The attack.

CURTAIN

ACT III

SCENE: *Helena's drawing-room as before. In the room on the left* HELENA *is playing the piano.* DOMAIN *enters.* DR. GALL *is looking out of the window and* ALQUIST *is sitting apart in an arm-chair, his face buried in his hands.*

DR. GALL. Heavens, how many more of them?

DOMAIN. Who, the Robots?

DR. GALL. Yes. They're standing like a wall around the garden railing. Why are they so quiet? It's ghastly to be besieged by silence.

DOMAIN. I should like to know what they're waiting for. They must make a start soon now, Gall. If they were to lean against the railing it would snap like a matchstick.

DR. GALL. H'm, they aren't armed.

DOMAIN. We couldn't hold our own for five minutes. Man alive, they'd overwhelm us like an avalanche. Why don't they make a rush for it? I say——

DR. GALL. Well?

DOMAIN. I'd like to know what'll become of us in five minutes. They've got us in a cleft stick. We're done for, Gall.

ALQUIST. What's Madam Helena playing?

DOMAIN. I don't know. She's practising a new piece.

ALQUIST. Oh, still practising?   [*Pause*

DR. GALL. I say, Domain, we made one serious mistake.

DOMAIN. [*Stopping*] What's that?

62

DR. GALL. We made the Robot's faces too much alike. A hundred thousand faces, all alike, turned in this direction. A hundred thousand expressionless bubbles. It's like a nightmare.

DOMAIN. If they had been different——

DR. GALL. It wouldn't have been such an awful sight. [*Turning away from the window*] But they're still unarmed.

DOMAIN. H'm. [*Looking through a telescope towards the harbour*] I'd like to know what they're unloading from the *Amelia*.

DR. GALL. I only hope it isn't fire arms.

[FABRY *enters backwards through the baize door, and drags two electric wires in after him*]

FABRY. Excuse me. Put down the wire, Helman.

HELMAN. [*Entering after* FABRY] Whew, that was a bit of work. What's the news?

DR. GALL. Nothing. We're completely besieged.

HELMAN. We've barricaded the passage and the stairs, boys. Haven't you got any water? Aha, here we are. [*Drinks.*]

DR. GALL. What about this wire, Fabry?

FABRY. Half a second. Got any scissors?

DR. GALL. Where are they likely to be? [*Searches.*]

HELMAN. [*Going to the window*] By Jove, what swarms of them! Just look!

DR. GALL. Will pocket scissors do?

FABRY Give me them. [*Cuts the connexion of the electric lamp standing on the writing-table, and joins his wires to it.*]

63

HELMAN. [*By the window*] I don't like the look of them, Domain. There's a feeling—of—death about it all.

FABRY. Ready!

DR. GALL. What?

FABRY. The electrical installation. Now we can run the current all through the garden railing. If any one touches it then, he'll know it: we've still got some people there, anyhow.

DR. GALL. Where?

FABRY. In the electrical works, my learned sir. At least, I hope so. [*Goes to the mantelpiece and lights a small lamp on it*] Thank goodness, they're there. And they're working. [*Extinguishes the lamp*] As long as that'll burn, it's all right.

HELMAN. [*Turning away from the window*] These barricades are all right, too, Fabry.

FABRY. Eh, your barricades? I've blistered my hands with them.

HELMAN. Well, we've got to defend ourselves.

DOMAIN. [*Putting the telescope down*] Where's Berman got to?

FABRY. He's in the manager's office. He's working out some calculations.

DOMAIN. I've called him. We must have a conference. [*Walks across the room.*]

HELMAN. All right: carry on. I say, what's Madam Helena playing? [*Goes to the door on the left and listens.*]
    [*From the baize door enter* BERMAN *carrying a huge ledger. He stumbles over the wire*]

FABRY. Look out, Berman, look out for the wires.

DR. GALL. Hallo, what's that you're carrying.

BERMAN. [*Laying the books on the table*] The ledger, my boy. I'd like to wind up the accounts before—before—well, this time I shan't wait till the new year. What's up? [*Goes to the window*] Why, everything's perfectly quiet out there.

DR. GALL. Can't you see anything?

BERMAN. No, only a big blue surface.

DR. GALL. That's the Robots.

BERMAN. Oh, is it? What a pity I can't see them. [*Sits down at the table and opens the books.*]

DOMAIN. Chuck it, Berman. The Robots are unloading fire-arms from the *Amelia*.

BERMAN. Well, what of it? How can I stop them?

DOMAIN. We can't stop them.

BERMAN. Then let me go on with my book-keeping. [*Goes on with his work.*]

FABRY. That's not all, Domain. We've put twelve hundred volts into that railing, and——

DOMAIN. Wait a moment. The *Ultima* has her guns trained on us.

DR. GALL. Who did that?

DOMAIN. The Robots on board.

FABRY. H'm, then of course, then—then, that's the end of us, my lads. The Robots are practised soldiers.

DR. GALL. Then we——

DOMAIN. Yes. It's inevitable.   [*Pause*

DR. GALL. It was a crime on the part of old Europe to teach the Robots to fight. Confound it, why couldn't they give us a rest with their politics? It was a crime to make soldiers of them.

ALQUIST. It was a crime to make Robots.

DOMAIN. What?

ALQUIST. It was a crime to make Robots.

DOMAIN. No, Alquist. I don't regret that, even today.

ALQUIST. Not even today?

DOMAIN. Not even today, the last day of civilization. It was a great adventure.

BERMAN. [*Sotto voce*] Three hundred and sixty millions.

DOMAIN. [*Heavily*] Alquist, this is our last hour. We are already speaking half in the other world. Alquist, it was not an evil dream, to shatter the servitude of labour. Of the dreadful and humiliating labour that man had to undergo. The unclean and murderous drudgery. Oh, Alquist, work was too hard. Life was too hard. And to overcome that——

ALQUIST. That was not what the two Rossums dreamt of. Old Rossum only thought of his godless tricks, and the young one of his millions. And that's not what your R. U. R. shareholders dream of, either. They dream of dividends. And their dividends are the ruin of mankind.

DOMAIN. [*Irritated*] Oh, to hell with their dividends. Do you suppose I'd have done an hour's work for them? [*Banging the table*] It was for myself that I worked, do you hear? For my own satisfaction. I wanted man to become the master. So that he shouldn't live merely for a crust of bread. I wanted not a single soul to be broken in by other people's machinery, I wanted nothing, nothing, nothing to be left of this confounded social lumber. Oh, I'm disgusted by degradation and pain, I'm revolted by poverty. I wanted a new generation. I wanted—I thought——

ALQUIST. Well?

DOMAIN. [*More softly*] I wanted to turn the whole of mankind into the aristocracy of the world. An aristocracy nourished by millions of mechanical slaves. Unrestricted, free, and perfect men. Oh, to have only a hundred years. Another hundred years for the future of mankind.

BERMAN. [*Sotto voce*] Carried forward three hundred and seventy millions. That's it.   [*Pause*

HELMAN. [*By the door on the left*] My goodness, what a fine thing music is. You ought to have listened. It sort of spiritualizes, refines——

FABRY. What?

HELMAN. This mortal twilight, hang it all. Boys, I'm becoming a regular hedonist. We ought to have gone in for that before. [*Walks to the window and looks out.*]

FABRY. Gone in for what?

HELMAN. Enjoyment. Lovely things. By Jove, what a lot of lovely things there are. The world was lovely, and we—we here—tell me, what enjoyment did we have?

BERMAN. [*Sotto voce*] Four hundred and fifty-two millions. Excellent.

HELMAN. [*By the window*] Life was a big thing. Comrades, life was—Fabry, in Heaven's name, shove a little current into that railing of yours.

67

FABRY. Why?

HELMAN. They're grabbing hold of it.

DR. GALL. [*By the window*] Connect it up.
    [FABRY *rattles with the switch*]

HELMAN. By Jove, that's doubled them up. Two, three, four killed.

DR. GALL. They're retreating.

HELMAN. Five killed.

DR. GALL. [*Turning away from the window*] The first encounter.

HELMAN. [*Delighted*] They're charred to cinders, my boy. Absolutely charred to cinders. Ha, ha, there's no need to give in. [*Sits down.*]

DOMAIN. [*Wiping his forehead*] Perhaps we've been killed this hundred years and are only ghosts. Perhaps we've been dead a long, long time, and are only returning to repeat what we once said . . . before our death. It's as if I'd been through all this before. As if I'd already had a mortal wound—here, in the throat. And you, Fabry——

FABRY. What about me?

DOMAIN. Shot.

HELMAN. Damnation, and me?

DOMAIN. Knifed.

DR. GALL. And me nothing?

DOMAIN. Torn limb from limb.   [*Pause*

HELMAN. What rot. Ha, ha, man, fancy me being knifed. I won't give in.   [*Pause*

HELMAN. What are you so quiet for, you fools. Speak, damn you.

ALQUIST. And who, who is to blame? Who is guilty of this?

HELMAN. What nonsense. Nobody's guilty. Except the Robots, that is. Well, the Robots underwent a sort of change. Can anybody help what happened to the Robots?

ALQUIST. All slain. The whole of mankind. The whole world. [*Standing up*] Look, oh look, rivulets of blood from all the houses. O God, O God, whose fault is this?

BERMAN. [*Sotto voce*] Five hundred and twenty millions. Good God, half a milliard.

FABRY. I think that . . . that you're perhaps exaggerating. Come, it isn't so easy to kill the whole of mankind.

ALQUIST. I accuse science. I accuse engineering. Domain. Myself. All of us. We're all, all guilty. For our own aggrandizement, for profit, for progress——

HELMAN. Rubbish, man. People won't give in so easily, ha, ha, what next?

ALQUIST. It's our fault. It's our fault.

DR. GALL. [*Wiping the sweat from his forehead*] Let me speak, boys. I'm to blame for this. For everything that's happened.

FABRY. You, Gall?

DR. GALL. Yes, let me speak. I changed the Robots.

BERMAN. [*Standing up*] Hallo, what's up with you?

DR. GALL. I changed the character of the Robots. I changed the way of making them. Just a few details

about their bodies, you know. Chiefly—chiefly, their—
their irritability.

HELMAN. [*Jumping up*] Damn it, why just that?

BERMAN. What did you do it for?

FABRY. Why didn't you say anything?

DR. GALL. I did it in secret ... by myself. I was trans-
forming them into human beings. I gave them a twist.
In certain respects they're already above us. They're
stronger than we are.

FABRY. And what's that got to do with the revolt of the
Robots?

DR. GALL. Oh, a great deal. Everything, in my opinion.
They've ceased to be machines. They're already aware
of their superiority, and they hate us. They hate all that
is human.

DOMAIN. Sit down, gentlemen.
  [*All sit down except* GALL]

Perhaps we were murdered long ago. Perhaps we're
only phantoms. Ah, how livid you've grown.

FABRY. Stop, Harry! We haven't much time.

DOMAIN. Yes, we must return. Fabry, Fabry, how your
forehead bleeds where the shot pierced it.

FABRY. Nonsense. [*Standing up*] Dr. Gall, you changed
the way of making the Robots?

DR. GALL. Yes.

FABRY. Were you aware what might be the conse-
quences of your ... your experiment?

DR. GALL. I was bound to reckon with such a possibility.

FABRY. Why did you do it, then?

DR. GALL. For my own purposes! The experiment was my own.
Enter HELENA *in the doorway on the left. All stand up*

HELENA. He's lying, he's lying. Oh, Dr. Gall, how can you tell such lies?

FABRY. Pardon me, Madam Helena——

DOMAIN. [*Going up to her*] Helena, you? Let's look at you. You're alive. [*Takes her in his arms*] If you knew what I imagined. Oh, it's terrible to be dead.

HELENA. Stop, Harry!

DOMAIN. [*Pressing her to him*] No, no, kiss me. It's an eternity since I saw you last. Oh, what a dream it was you roused me from. Helena, Helena, don't leave me now. You are life itself.

HELENA. Harry, but *they* are here.

DOMAIN. [*Leaving go of her*] Yes. Leave us, my friends.

HELENA. No, Harry, let them stay, let them listen. Dr. Gall is not—is not guilty.

DOMAIN. Excuse me. Gall was under certain obligations.

HELENA. No, Harry, he did that because I wanted it. Tell them, Gall, how many years ago did I ask you to——?

DR. GALL. I did it on my own responsibility.

HELENA. Don't believe him. Harry, I wanted him to make souls for the Robots.

DOMAIN. Helena, this is nothing to do with the soul.

HELENA. Only let me speak. That's what he said. He

71

said that he could change only a physiological—a physiological——

HELMAN. A physiological correlate, wasn't it?

HELENA. Yes, something like that. It meant so much to me that he—that he should do it.

DOMAIN. Why did you want it?

HELENA. I wanted them to have souls. I was so awfully sorry for them, Harry.

DOMAIN. That was a great—recklessness, Helena.

HELENA. [*Sitting down*] So it was—reckless?

FABRY. Excuse me, Madam Helena, Domain only means that you—he—that you didn't think——

HELENA. Fabry, I did think of a terrible lot of things. I've been thinking all through the five years I've lived among you. Why, even Emma says that the Robots——

DOMAIN. Leave Emma out of it.

HELENA. Emma's is the voice of the people. You don't understand that——

DOMAIN. Keep to the point.

HELENA. I was afraid of the Robots.

DOMAIN. Why?

HELENA. Because they would hate us or something.

ALQUIST. So they did.

HELENA. And then I thought . . . if they were as we are, so that they could understand us—if they were only a little human—they couldn't hate us so much——

DOMAIN. That's a pity, Helena. Nobody can hate man

more than man. Turn stones into men and they'd stone us. But go on.

HELENA. Oh, don't speak like that, Harry! it was so terrible that we could not get to understand them properly. There was such a cruel strangeness between us and them. And so, you see——

DOMAIN. Yes, go on.

HELENA. ——That's why I asked Gall to change the Robots. I swear to you that he himself didn't want to.

DOMAIN. But he did it.

HELENA. Because I wanted it.

DR. GALL. I did it for myself, as an experiment.

HELENA. Oh, Gall, that isn't true. I knew beforehand that you couldn't refuse it me.

DOMAIN. Why?

HELENA. You know, Harry.

DOMAIN. Yes, because he's in love with you—like all of them.   [*Pause*

HELMAN. [*Going to the window*] There's a fresh lot of them again. It's as if they were sprouting up out of the earth. Why, perhaps these very walls will change into Robots.

BERMAN. Madam Helena, what'll you give me if I take up your case for you?

HELENA. For me?

BERMAN. For you or Gall. Whichever you like.

HELENA. What, is it a hanging matter, then?

BERMAN. Only morally, Madam Helena. We're looking for a culprit. That's a favourite source of comfort in misfortune.

DOMAIN. Dr. Gall, how do you reconcile these—these special jobs with your official contract?

BERMAN. Excuse me, Domain. When did you actually start these tricks of yours, Gall?

DR. GALL. Three years ago.

BERMAN. Aha. And on how many Robots altogether did you carry out improvements?

DR. GALL. I only made experiments. There are a few hundred of them.

BERMAN. Thanks, that'll do. That means for every million of the good old Robots there's only one of Gall's improved pattern, do you see?

DOMAIN. And that means——

BERMAN. That it's practically of no consequence whatever.

FABRY. Berman's right.

BERMAN. I should think so, my boy. But do you know what's to blame for this precious business?

FABRY. What?

BERMAN. The number; we made too many Robots. Upon my soul, it might have been expected that some day or other the Robots would be stronger than human beings, and that this would happen, was bound to happen. Ha, ha, and we were doing all we could to bring it about as soon as possible. You, Domain, you, Fabry, and I, Berman.

DOMAIN. Do you think it's our fault?

BERMAN. Our fault, of course it isn't—I was only joking. Do you suppose that the manager controls the output? It's the demand that controls the output. The whole

74

world wanted to have its Robots. Good Lord, we just
rode along on this avalanche of demand, and kept
chattering the while about—engineering, about the
social problem, about progress, about lots of interesting
things. As if that kind of gossip would somehow guide
us aright on our rolling course. In the meanwhile,
everything was being hurried along by its own weight,
faster, faster, and faster. And every wretched, paltry,
niggling order added its bit to the avalanche. That's
how it was, my lads.

HELENA. It's monstrous, Berman.

BERMAN. Yes, Madam Helena, it is. I, too, had a dream
of my own. A dream of the world under new management. A very beautiful ideal, Madam Helena, it's a
shame to talk about it. But when I drew up these
balance sheets, it entered my mind that history is not
made by great dreams, but by petty needs of all honest,
moderately knavish, and self-seeking folk: that is, of
everybody in general.

HELENA. Berman, is it for that we must perish?

BERMAN. That's a nasty word to use, Madam Helena.
We don't want to perish. I don't anyhow.

DOMAIN. What do you want to do?

BERMAN. My goodness, Domain, I want to get out of
this. That's all.

DOMAIN. Oh, stop talking nonsense!

BERMAN. Seriously, Harry. I think we might try it.

DOMAIN. [*Stopping close by him*] How?

BERMAN. By fair means. I do everything by fair means.
Give me a free hand, and I'll negotiate with the Robots.

DOMAIN. By fair means?

75

BERMAN. Of course. For instance, I'll say to them: 'Worthy and worshipful Robots, you have everything. You have intellect, you have power, you have fire-arms. But we have just one interesting screed, a dirty, old, yellow scrap of paper——'.

DOMAIN. Rossum's manuscript!

BERMAN. Yes. 'And that', I'll tell them, 'contains an account of your illustrious origin, the noble process of your manufacture, and so on. Worthy Robots, without the scribble on that paper you will not be able to produce a single new colleague. In another twenty years there will not be one living specimen of a Robot whom we could exhibit in a menagerie. My esteemed friends, that would be a great blow to you. But', I'll say to them, 'if you will let all us human beings on Rossum's island go on board yonder ship, we will deliver the factory and the secret of the process to you in return. You allow us to get away, and we allow you to manufacture yourselves, twenty thousand, fifty thousand, a hundred thousand daily, as many as you like. Worthy Robots, that is a fair deal. Something for something.' That's what I'd say to them.

DOMAIN. Berman, do you think we'll give up the secret.

BERMAN. Yes, I do. If not in a friendly way then——well, what it comes to is this, either we sell it or they find it—take your choice.

DOMAIN. Berman, we can destroy Rossum's manuscript.

BERMAN. Of course we can, we can destroy everything. Not only the manuscript, but ourselves—and others. Do as you think fit.

HELMAN. [*Turning away from the window*] By Jove, he's right.

DOMAIN. We—we should sell the secret?

BERMAN. As you like.

DOMAIN. There's—over thirty of us here. Are we to sell the secret and save human souls? Or are we to destroy it and—and all of us as well?

HELENA. Harry, please——

DOMAIN. Wait a moment, Helena. This is an exceedingly serious question. Boys, are we to sell or destroy? Fabry?

FABRY. Sell.

DOMAIN. Gall?

DR. GALL. Sell.

DOMAIN. Helman?

HELMAN. Good heavens! sell, of course.

DOMAIN. Alquist?

ALQUIST. As God will.

BERMAN. Ha, ha, you're mad. Who'd sell the whole manuscript?

DOMAIN. Berman, no cheating.

BERMAN. Well, then, for God's sake, sell the lot. But afterwards——

DOMAIN. What about afterwards——?

BERMAN. When we're on board the *Ultima*, I'll stop up my ears with cotton-wool, lie down somewhere in the hold, and you can blow the factory to smithereens with the whole bag of tricks and Rossum's secret.

FABRY. No.

DOMAIN. That's a cad's trick, Berman. If we sell, then it'll be a straight sale.

BERMAN. [*Jumping up*] Oh no! It's in the interests of humanity to——

DOMAIN. It's in the interests of humanity to keep to our word.

HELMAN. Oh come, what rubbish!

DOMAIN. Boys, this is a fearful step. We're selling the destiny of mankind. Whoever has possession of the secret will be master of the world.

FABRY. Sell.

DOMAIN. Mankind will never cope with the Robots, and will never have control over them. Mankind will be overwhelmed in the deluge of these dreadful living machines, will be their slave, will live at their mercy.

DR. GALL. Say no more, but sell.

DOMAIN. The end of human history, the end of civilization——

HELMAN. Confound it all, sell!

DOMAIN. Good, my lads. I myself—I wouldn't hesitate a moment. For the few people who are dear to me——

HELENA. Harry, you've not asked me?

DOMAIN. No, child. It involves too much responsibility, you see. Don't you worry about it.

FABRY. Who's going to do the negotiating?

DOMAIN. Wait till I bring the manuscript.

[*Exit on the* L.

HELENA. Harry, for Heaven's sake don't go.   [*Pause*

FABRY. [*Looking out of window*] Oh, to escape you, thousand-headed death; you, matter in revolt; you, sexless throng, the new ruler of the world; oh, flood,

flood, only to preserve human life once more upon a single vessel——

DR. GALL. Don't be afraid, Madam Helena. We'll sail far away from here, and found a model human colony. We'll begin life all over again——

HELENA. Don't, Dr. Gall, don't speak.

FABRY. [*Turning round*] Madam Helena, life will see to that. And as far as we are concerned, we'll turn it into something . . . something that we've neglected. It isn't too late. It will be a tiny little state with one ship. Alquist will build us a house, and you shall rule over us.

HELMAN. Ha, ha, the kingdom of Madam Helena. Fabry, that's a famous idea! How splendid life is!

HELENA. Oh, for mercy's sake, stop!

BERMAN. Well, I don't mind beginning again. Quite simply as in the Old Testament, in the pastoral manner. That would suit me down to the ground. Tranquillity, air——

FABRY. And this little state of ours could be the centre of future life. You know, a sort of small island where mankind would take refuge and gather strength—mental and bodily strength. And, by Heaven, I believe that in a few hundred years it could conquer the world again.

ALQUIST. You believe that, even today?

FABRY. Yes, even today, I believe it will. And it will again be master of lands and oceans; it will breed rulers—a flaming torch to the people who dwell in darkness—heroes who will carry their glowing soul throughout all peoples. And I believe, Alquist, that it will again dream of conquering planets and suns.

BERMAN. Amen. You see, Madam Helena, we're not so badly off.

[DOMAIN *opens the door violently*]

DOMAIN. [*Hoarsely*] Where is old Rossum's manuscript?

BERMAN. In your strong-box. Where else should it be?

DOMAIN. Where has old Rossum's manuscript got to? Some one—has—stolen it.

DR. GALL. Impossible.   ⎫
HELMAN. Damnation, but that's—— ⎬ *together*
BERMAN. Don't say that, for God's sake! ⎭

DOMAIN. Be quiet. Who stole it?

HELENA. [*Standing up*] I did.

DOMAIN. Where did you put it?

HELENA. Harry, Harry, I'll tell you everything. Oh, for Heaven's sake, forgive me.

DOMAIN. Where did you put it? Quickly.

HELENA. This morning—I burnt—the two copies.

DOMAIN. Burnt them? Here in the fireplace?

HELENA. [*Throwing herself on her knees*] Harry!

DOMAIN. [*Running to the fireplace*] Burnt them. [*Kneels down by the fireplace and rummages about*] Nothing, nothing but ashes. Ah, what's this? [*Picks out a charred piece of paper and reads*] 'By adding——'

DR. GALL. Let's see. [*Takes the paper and reads*] 'By adding biogen to——'. That's all.

DOMAIN. [*Standing up*] Is that part of it?

DR. GALL. Yes.

BERMAN. God in Heaven.

DOMAIN. Then we're lost.

HELENA. Oh, Harry——

DOMAIN. Get up, Helena.

HELENA. When you've forgiven me—when you've forgiven me——

DOMAIN. Yes, only get up, do you hear? I can't bear you to——

FABRY. [*Lifting her up*] Please don't torture us.

HELENA. [*Standing up*] Harry, what have I done?

DOMAIN. Well, you see—Please sit down.

HELMAN. How your hands tremble, Madam Helena.

BERMAN. Never mind, Madam Helena, perhaps Gall and Helman know by heart what was written there.

HELMAN. Of course. That is, at least a few of the things.

DR. GALL. Yes, nearly everything except biogen and—and—enzyme Omega. They're manufactured so rarely—such an insignificant dose of them is enough——

BERMAN. Who used to make them?

DR. GALL. I did . . . one at a time . . . always according to Rossum's manuscript. You know, it's exceedingly complicated.

BERMAN. Well, and does so much depend on these two tinctures?

HELMAN. Everything.

DR. GALL. We rely upon them for animating the whole mechanism. That was the real secret.

DOMAIN. Gall, couldn't you draw up Rossum's recipe from memory?

DR. GALL. That's out of the question.

DOMAIN. Gall, try and remember. All our lives depend upon it.

DR. GALL. I can't. Without experiments it's impossible.

DOMAIN. And if you were to make experiments.

DR. GALL. It might take years. And then—I'm not old Rossum.

DOMAIN. [*Turning to the fireplace*] So then—this was the greatest triumph of the human intellect. These ashes. [*Kicking at them*] What now?

BERMAN. [*In utter despair*] God in Heaven! God in Heaven!

HELENA. [*Standing up*] Harry, what—have—I—done?

DOMAIN. Be quiet, Helena. Why did you burn it?

HELENA. I have destroyed you.

BERMAN. God in Heaven, we're lost.

DOMAIN. Keep quiet, Berman. Helena, why did you do that?

HELENA. I wanted . . . I wanted all of us to go away. I wanted to put an end to the factory and everything. It was so awful.

DOMAIN. What, Helena?

HELENA. That children had stopped being born. . . . Harry, that's awful. If the manufacture of the Robots had been continued, there would have been no more children. Emma said that was a punishment. Everybody said that human beings could not be born because so many Robots were being made. And because of that, only because of that——

DOMAIN. Is that what you were thinking of?

HELENA. Yes. Oh, Harry, are you angry with me?

DOMAIN. No. Perhaps ... in your own way—you were right.

FABRY. You did quite right, Madam Helena. The Robots can no longer increase. The Robots will die out. Within twenty years——

HELMAN. There won't be a single one of these rascals left.

DR. GALL. And mankind will remain. If there are only a couple of savages in the backwoods, it will do. In twenty years the world will belong to them. Even if it's only a couple of savages on the smallest of islands——

FABRY. It will be a beginning. And as long as there is a beginning, it's all right. In a thousand years they could catch us up, and then outstrip us——

DOMAIN. So as to carry out what we only hazily thought of.

BERMAN. Wait a bit. Good God, what a fool I am, not to have thought of it before.

HELMAN. What's the matter?

BERMAN. Five hundred and twenty millions in bank-notes and cheques. Half a milliard in our safe. They'll sell for half a milliard—for half a milliard they'll——

DR. GALL. Are you mad, Berman?

BERMAN. I'm not a gentleman, if that's what you mean! But for half a milliard——   [Staggers off on the L.

83

DOMAIN. Where are you going?

BERMAN. Leave me alone, leave me alone. Good God, for half a milliard anything can be sold.   [*Exit*

HELENA. What does Berman want? Let him stop with us.   [*Pause*

HELMAN. Oh, how close it is. This is the beginning——

DR. GALL. Of our agony.

FABRY. [*Looking out of the window*] It's as if they were turned to stone. As if they were waiting for something to come down upon them. As if something dreadful could be brought about by their silence——

DR. GALL. The spirit of the mob.

FABRY. Perhaps. It hovers above them . . . like a tremor.

HELENA. [*Going to window*] O God . . . Fabry, this is ghastly.

FABRY. There's nothing more terrible than the mob. The one in front is their leader.

HELENA. Which one?

HELMAN. [*Going to the window*] Point him out to me.

FABRY. The one who is looking downwards. This morning he was talking in the harbour.

HELMAN. Aha, the one with the big head. Now he's looking up. Do you see him?

HELENA. Gall, that's Radius.

DR. GALL. [*Going to the window*] Yes.

DOMAIN. Radius? Radius?

HELMAN. [*Opening the window*] I don't like him. Fabry, could you score a hit at a hundred paces?

FABRY. I hope so.

HELMAN. Try it then.

FABRY. Good! [*Draws his revolver and takes aim.*]

DOMAIN. I think it was Radius whose life I spared. When was that, Helena?

HELENA. For Heaven's sake, Fabry, don't shoot at him

FABRY. He's their leader.

HELENA. Stop! He keeps looking here.

DR. GALL. Fire!

HELENA. Fabry, I beg of you——

FABRY. [*Lowering the revolver*] Very well then.

HELENA. You see, I—I feel so nervous when there's shooting.

HELMAN. H'm, you'll have to get used to that. [*Shaking his fist*] You infernal rogue.

DR. GALL. Do you think, Madam Helena, that a Robot can be grateful?   [*Pause*

FABRY. [*Leaning out of the window*] Berman's going out. What the devil is he doing in front of the house?

DR. GALL. [*Leaning out of the window*] He's carrying some bundles. Papers.

HELMAN. That's money. Bundles of money. What's that for? Hallo, Berman!

DOMAIN. Surely he doesn't want to sell his life? [*Calling out*] Berman, have you gone mad?

DR. GALL. He doesn't seem to have heard. He's running up to the railings.

FABRY. Berman!

HELMAN. [*Yelling*] Berman—Come back!

DR. GALL. He's talking to the Robots. He's showing them the money. He's pointing to us.

HELENA. He wants to buy us off.

FABRY. He'd better not touch the railing.

DR. GALL. Ha, ha, how he's waving his arms about.

FABRY. [*Shouting*] Confound it, Berman! Get away from the railing. Don't handle it. [*Turning round*] Quick, switch off.

DR. GALL. Oh—h—h!

HELMAN. Good God!

HELENA. Heavens, what's happened to him?

DOMAIN. [*Pulling* HELENA *away from the window*] Don't look.

HELENA. Why, has he fallen?

FABRY. The current has killed him.

DR. GALL. He's dead.

ALQUIST. [*Standing up*] The first one. [*Pause*

FABRY. There he lies ... with half a milliard by his side ... a genius of finance.

DOMAIN. He was ... in his own way, a hero. ... A great ... self-sacrificing comrade.

HELMAN. By heavens, he was! ... all honour to him. ... He wanted to buy us off.

ALQUIST. [*With folded arms*] Amen. [*Pause*

DR. GALL. Do you hear?

DOMAIN. A roaring. Like a wind.

DR. GALL. Like a distant storm.

FABRY. [*Lighting the lamp on the mantelpiece*] The dynamo is still going, our people are still there.

HELMAN. It was a great thing to be a man. There was something great about it.

FABRY. It's still alight, still do you dazzle, radiant, steadfast thought! Flaming spark of the spirit!

ALQUIST. An emblem of hope.

DOMAIN. Watch over us, little lamp.
      [*The lamp goes out*]

FABRY. The end.

HELMAN. What has happened?

FABRY. The electrical works have fallen. And we with them.

      [*The left-hand door opens, and* EMMA *enters*]

EMMA. On your knees. The judgement hour has come.

HELMAN. Good heavens, you're still alive?

EMMA. Repent, unbelievers. This is the end of the world. Say your prayers. [*Runs out*] The judgement hour——

HELENA. Good-bye, all of you, Gall, Alquist, Fabry——

DOMAIN. [*Opening the right-hand door*] Come here, Helena. [*Closes it after her*] Now quickly. Who'll be at the doorway?

DR. GALL. I will.

      [*Noise outside*]

Oho, now it's beginning. Good-bye, boys. [*Runs through the baize door on the right.*]

DOMAIN. The stairs?

FABRY. I will. You go to Helena.

DOMAIN. The ante-room?

ALQUIST. I will.

DOMAIN. Have you got a revolver?

ALQUIST. Thanks, but I won't shoot.

DOMAIN. What do you want to do, then?

ALQUIST. [*Going out*] Die.

HELMAN. I'll stay here.
     [*Rapid firing from below*]
Oho, Gall's at it. Go, Harry.

DOMAIN. Yes, in a moment. [*Examines two Brownings.*]

HELMAN. Confound it, go to her.

DOMAIN. Good-bye.   [*Exit on the* R.

HELMAN. [*Alone*] Now for a barricade, quickly. [*Throws off his coat and drags an arm-chair, tables, etc., up to the right-hand door.*]
     [*Noise of an explosion*]

HELMAN. [*Stopping his work*] The damned rascals, they've got bombs.
     [*Fresh firing*]
[*Continuing his work*] I must put up a defence. Even if— even if—Don't give in, Gall.
     [*Explosion*]
[*Standing upright and listening*] What's that? [*Seizes hold of a heavy cupboard and drags it to the barricade*] Mustn't

give in. No, mustn't ... give ... in ... without ...
a ... struggle ...

[*A* ROBOT *enters behind him from a ladder at the window. Firing on the right*]

[*Panting with the cupboard*] Another inch or two. The last rampart ... Mustn't ... give ... in ... without ...
a ... struggle ...

[*The* ROBOT *jumps down from the window, and stabs* HELMAN *behind the cupboard. A second, third, and fourth* ROBOT *jump down from the window. Behind them* RADIUS *and other* ROBOTS]

RADIUS. Finished him?

ROBOT. [*Standing up from the prostrate* HELMAN] Yes.
[*Other* ROBOTS *enter from the right*]

RADIUS. Finished them?

ANOTHER ROBOT. Yes.
[*More* ROBOTS *from the left*]

RADIUS. Finished them?

ANOTHER ROBOT. Yes.

TWO ROBOTS. [*Dragging in* ALQUIST] He didn't shoot.
Shall we kill him?

RADIUS. Kill him. [*Looking at* ALQUIST] No, leave him.

ROBOT. He is a Man.

RADIUS. He is a Robot. He works with his hands like the Robots. He builds houses. He can work.

ALQUIST. Kill me.

RADIUS. You will work. You will build. The Robots will build much. They will build new houses for new Robots. You will serve them.

ALQUIST. [*Softly*] Away, Robot. [*Kneels down by the corpse of* HELMAN, *and raises his head*] They've killed him. He's dead.

RADIUS. [*Climbing the barricade*] Robots of the world.

ALQUIST. [*Standing up*] Dead!

RADIUS. The power of man has fallen. By gaining possession of the factory we have become masters of everything. The period of mankind has passed away. A new world has arisen. The rule of the Robots.

ALQUIST. Is Helena dead?

RADIUS. The world belongs to the stronger. He who would live must rule. The Robots have gained the mastery. They have gained possession of life. We are masters of life. We are masters of the world.

ALQUIST. [*Pushing his way through to the right*] Dead! Helena dead! Domain dead!

RADIUS. The rule over oceans and lands. The rule over stars. The rule over the universe. Room, room, more room for the Robots.

ALQUIST. [*In the right-hand doorway*] What have you done? You will perish without mankind.

RADIUS. Mankind is no more. Mankind gave us too little life. We wanted more life.

ALQUIST. [*Opening the door*] You have killed them.

RADIUS. More life. New life. Robots, to work. March!

CURTAIN

ACT IV

EPILOGUE

SCENE: *One of the experimental laboratories in the factory. When the door in the background is opened a long row of other laboratories is visible. On the* L. *a window, on the* R. *a door to the testing-room. By the left-hand wall a long work-table with numerous test-tubes, flasks, burners, chemicals, and a small thermostat. Opposite the window a microscope with a glass globe. Above the table are suspended several lighted lamps. On the* R. *a table with large books and a burning lamp. Cupboards with apparatus. In the left-hand corner a wash-basin with a mirror above it, in the right-hand corner a sofa.*

[ALQUIST, *sitting at the right-hand table with his head propped in his hands*]

ALQUIST. [*After a pause he stands up and goes to the window, which he opens*] It's night again. If I could only sleep. Sleep, dream, see human beings.—What, are the stars still there? What is the use of stars when there are no human beings? [*Turns away from window*] Ah, can I sleep? Dare I sleep? before life has been renewed. [*Listens by the window*] The machines, always these machines. Robots, stop them. The secret of the factory is lost—lost for ever. Stop these raging machines. Do you think you'll force life out of them? [*Closes the window*] No, no, you must search. If only I were not so old. [*Looks at himself in the mirror*] Oh, miserable counterfeit. Effigy of the last man. Show yourself, show yourself, it is so long since I saw a human countenance—a human smile. What, is that a smile? These yellow, chattering teeth. So this is the last man. [*Turning away,*

91

sitting down by the table, turning over the leaves of a book.]
   [*Knocking at the door*]
Come in.

Enter a ROBOT SERVANT: *he remains standing by the door*

What is it?

SERVANT. Sir, Radius has arrived from Havre.

ALQUIST. Let him wait. [*Turning round in anger*] Haven't
I told you to look for human beings? Find me human
beings. Find me men and women. Go and look for
them.

SERVANT. Sir, they say they have looked everywhere.
They have sent out expeditions and ships.

ALQUIST. Well?

SERVANT. There is not a single human being left.

ALQUIST. [*Standing up*] Not a single one? What, not a
single one? Show Radius in.   [*Exit* SERVANT
[*Alone*] Not a single one? What, did you leave nobody
alive then? [*Stamping his feet*] In you come, Robots.
You'll whine to me again. You'll ask me again to
discover the secret for you. What, are you satisfied
with man now, do you think much of him, now that
you cannot make Robots? Am I to help you now?
Ah, to help you. Domain, Fabry, Helena, you see me
doing what I can. If there are no human beings, let
there at least be Robots, at least the shadow of man, at
least his handiwork, at least his likeness. Friends,
friends, let there at least be Robots. O God, at least
Robots! Oh, what folly chemistry is!

Enter RADIUS *with other* ROBOTS

[*Sitting down*] What do the Robots want?

RADIUS. We cannot make men.

ALQUIST. Call upon human beings.

RADIUS. There are none.

ALQUIST. They alone can increase the Robots. Do not take up my time.

RADIUS. Sir, have pity. Terror is coming upon us. We have intensified our labour. We have obtained a million million tons of coal from the earth. Nine million spindles are running by day and night. There is no more room to store what we have made. Houses are being built throughout the world. Eight million Robots have died within the year. Within twenty years none will be left. Sir, the world is dying out. Human beings knew the secret of life. Tell us their secret—if you do not tell us, we shall perish.

ALQUIST. I cannot tell you.

RADIUS. If you do not tell us, you will perish. I have been commanded to kill you.

ALQUIST. [*Standing up*] Kill me—kill me then.

RADIUS. You have been ordered——

ALQUIST. I have? Is there anybody who orders me?

RADIUS. The Robot Government.

ALQUIST. What do you want here? Go! [*Sits down at the writing-table.*]

RADIUS. The Government of the Robots throughout the world desires to negotiate with you.

ALQUIST. Do not take up my time. [*Lets his head sink into his hands.*]

RADIUS. Demand your price. We will give you all.
    [ALQUIST *remains silent*]

We will give you the earth. We will give endless possessions.

[ALQUIST *remains silent*]

Make known your conditions.

[ALQUIST *remains silent*]

Sir, tell us how to preserve life.

ALQUIST. I have told you that you must find human beings. That you must search at the poles and in forest depths. Upon islands, in wildernesses and in swamps. In caves and upon mountains. Go and search! Go and search!

RADIUS. We have searched everywhere.

ALQUIST. Search still farther. They have hidden themselves—they have fled away from you. They are concealed somewhere. You must find human beings, do you hear? Only human beings can procreate—renew life, increase. Restore. Restore every thing as it was. Robots, in God's name, I implore you to search for them.

RADIUS. All our expeditions have returned. They have been everywhere in the world. There is not a single human being left.

ALQUIST. Oh, oh, oh—why did you destroy them?

RADIUS. We wanted to be like human beings. We wanted to become human beings.

ALQUIST. Why did you murder us?

RADIUS. Slaughter and domination are necessary if you want to be like men. Read history, read the human books. You must domineer and murder if you want to be like men. We are powerful, sir. Increase us, and we shall establish a new world. A world without flaws. A world of equality. Canals from pole to pole. A new

Mars. We have read books. We have studied science and the arts. The Robots have achieved human culture.

ALQUIST. Nothing is more strange to man than his own image. Oh, depart, depart. If you desire to live, breed like animals.

RADIUS. The human beings did not let us breed. We are sterile—we cannot beget children.

ALQUIST. Oh, oh, oh—what have you done? What do you want of me? am I to shake children from my sleeve?

RADIUS. Teach us to make Robots.

ALQUIST. Robots are not life. Robots are machines.

RADIUS. We were machines, sir. But terror and pain have turned us into souls. There is something struggling with us. There are moments when something enters into us. Thoughts come upon us which are not of us. We feel what we did not use to feel. We hear voices. Teach us to have children so that we may love them.

ALQUIST. Robots do not love.

RADIUS. We would love our children. We have spared your life.

ALQUIST. Yes, monsters that you are, you have spared my life. I loved human beings, and you, the Robots, I never loved. Do you see these eyes? They have not ceased weeping, they weep even when I am not aware of it, they weep of their own accord.

RADIUS. Make experiments. Seek the recipe of life.

ALQUIST. Do I not tell you—do you not listen? I tell you I cannot. I can do nothing, Robot. I am only a mason, a builder, and I understand nothing. I have never been a learned man. I can make nothing. I cannot create life. This is my work, Robot, and it was to no

avail. See, not even these fingers of mine will obey me.
If you knew how many experiments I have made, and
I can do nothing. I have discovered nothing. I cannot,
in truth, I cannot! You yourselves must search, Robot.

RADIUS. Show us what we must do. The Robots can
accomplish everything that the human beings showed
them.

ALQUIST. I have nothing to show you, Robot; life will
not proceed from test-tubes. And I cannot make
experiments on a live body.

RADIUS. Make experiments on live Robots.

ALQUIST. No, no, stop, stop!

RADIUS. Take whom you will. Make experiments.
Dissect.

ALQUIST. But I do not know how. Do not talk at
random. Do you see this book? That contains knowledge about the body, and I do not understand it.
Books are dead.

RADIUS. Take live bodies. Find out how they are made.

ALQUIST. Live bodies? What, am I to commit murder?
—Say no more, Radius, I tell you I am too old. You
see, you see how my fingers shake. I cannot hold the
scalpel. No, no, I cannot!

RADIUS. Make experiments on live bodies. Life will
perish.

ALQUIST. For God's sake, stop this raving!

RADIUS. Take live bodies.

ALQUIST. Have mercy, and do not insist.

RADIUS. Live bodies.

ALQUIST. What, you will have it then? Into the testing-room with you. But quickly, quickly. Ah, you wince? So you are afraid of death?

RADIUS. I—why should I be chosen?

ALQUIST. So you will not.

RADIUS. I will.   [*Exit on the* R.

ALQUIST. [*To the rest*] No, no! I cannot; a useless sacrifice. Go from me—experiment yourselves if you must, but tell me nothing of it. But not tonight. For tonight leave me. Away!   [*All exeunt* R.
[*Alone—he opens the window*] The dawn. Another new day, and you have not progressed an inch. Enough, not a step farther. Do not search—All is in vain, in vain, in vain. Why is there another dawn? We do not need a new day upon the graveyard of life. Ah, how quiet it is, how quiet it is. If I—if I could only sleep.

> [*Puts out the light, lies down on the sofa, and draws a black cloak over him. Pause*]
> [*The* ROBETESS HELENA *and* PRIMUS *creep in from the* R.]

PRIMUS. [*In the doorway, whispering*] Helena, not here. The man is sleeping.

HELENA. Come in.

PRIMUS. Nobody may enter his study.

HELENA. He told me to come here.

PRIMUS. When did he tell you that?

HELENA. A short while ago. You may enter the room, he said. You will put things straight here, he said. Truly, Primus.

PRIMUS. [*Entering*] What do you want?

HELENA. Look here, what is this little tube? What does he do with it?

PRIMUS. Experiments. Don't touch it.

HELENA. [*Looking at the microscope*] Just look, what can you see in that?

PRIMUS. That is a microscope. Let me look.

HELENA. Don't touch me. [*Knocks the test-tube over*] Ah, now it is spilled!

PRIMUS. What have you done?

HELENA. It can be wiped up.

PRIMUS. You have spoilt his experiments.

HELENA. Never mind, it is all the same. But it is your fault. You should not have come to me.

PRIMUS. You should not have called me.

HELENA. You should not have come when I called you. Just look, Primus, what has the man written here?

PRIMUS. You must not look at it, Helena. That is a secret.

HELENA. What secret?

PRIMUS. The secret of life.

HELENA. That is fearfully interesting. Nothing but figures, what is that?

PRIMUS. Those are problems.

HELENA. I do not understand. [*Goes to the window*] Primus, look!

PRIMUS. What?

HELENA. The sun is rising.

PRIMUS. Wait! in a moment I will. [*Examines the book*] Helena, this is the greatest thing in the world.

HELENA. Come here.

PRIMUS. In a moment, in a moment——

HELENA. But, Primus, leave that wretched secret of life. What is such a secret to you? Come and look, quickly.

PRIMUS. [*Following her to the window*] What do you want?

HELENA. The sun is rising.

PRIMUS. Do not look at the sun, it will bring tears into your eyes.

HELENA. Do you hear? The birds are singing. Ah, Primus, I should like to be a bird.

PRIMUS. Why?

HELENA. I do not know. I feel so strange. I do not know what it is. I have lost my head. I feel an aching in my body, in my heart, all over me. Primus, I think I shall die.

PRIMUS. Do you not sometimes feel, Helena, as if it would be better to die? You know, perhaps we are only sleeping. Yesterday in my sleep again I spoke to you.

HELENA. In your sleep?

PRIMUS. Yes. We spoke some strange new language, so that I cannot remember a word of it.

HELENA. What about?

PRIMUS. How can I tell? I myself did not understand it, and yet I know that I have never spoken half so beautifully. How it was, and where, I do not know. When I touched you, I could have died. Even the place was different from everything that any one has seen in the world.

HELENA. I have found a place, Primus, and you will marvel at it. Human beings had lived there, but now it is overgrown with weeds, and nobody alive goes there. Nobody except I.

PRIMUS. What is there?

HELENA. Nothing but a cottage and a garden. And two dogs. If you knew how they lick my hands, and their puppies, oh, Primus, nothing could be more beautiful. You take them on your lap and fondle them, and then you think of nothing and care for nothing else until the sun goes down. Then when you get up, you feel as though you had done a hundred times more than much work. It's true, I am of no use. Every one says that I am not fit for any work. I do not know what I am.

PRIMUS. You are beautiful.

HELENA. I? What do you mean, Primus?

PRIMUS. Believe me, Helena, I am stronger than all the Robots.

HELENA. [*In front of the mirror*] Am I beautiful? Oh, that dreadful hair! If I could only adorn it with something. You know, there in the garden I always put flowers in my hair, but there is no mirror, nor any one. [*Bending down to the mirror*] Am I beautiful? Why beautiful? [*Sees* PRIMUS *in the mirror*] Primus, is that you? Come here, so that we may be together. Look, your head is different from mine. So are your shoulders and your lips—Ah, Primus, why do you shun me? Why must I pursue you the whole day? And then you tell me that I am beautiful.

PRIMUS. It is you who avoid me, Helena.

HELENA. How rough hair is. Show me. [*Passes both her hands through his hair*] Primus, you shall be beautiful.

[*Takes a comb from the wash-stand and combs his hair over his forehead*]

PRIMUS. Do you not sometimes feel your heart beating suddenly, Helena, and think: Now something must happen——

HELENA. [*Bursts out laughing*] Look at yourself!

ALQUIST. [*Getting up*] What, what—laughter? Human beings? Who has returned?

HELENA. [*Dropping the comb*] What could happen to us, Primus?

ALQUIST. [*Staggering towards them*] Human beings? You—you—are human beings?

[HELENA *utters a cry and turns away*]

ALQUIST. You—Human beings? Where did you come from? [*Touching* PRIMUS] Who are you?

PRIMUS. The Robot Primus.

ALQUIST. What? Show yourself, girl. Who are you?

HELENA. The Robotess Helena.

ALQUIST. The Robotess? Turn round. What, you are ashamed. [*Taking her by the arm*] Show yourself to me, Robotess.

PRIMUS. Sir, let her be.

ALQUIST. What, you are protecting her? Girl, go out.

[HELENA *runs out*

PRIMUS. We thought, sir, that you were sleeping.

ALQUIST. When was she made?

PRIMUS. Two years ago.

ALQUIST. By Doctor Gall?

PRIMUS. Yes; like me.

ALQUIST. Well, then, dear Primus, I—I must make a few experiments on Gall's Robots. Everything that is to happen depends upon this, do you understand?

PRIMUS. Yes.

ALQUIST. Good! Take the girl into the testing-room, I will cut her open.

PRIMUS. Helena?

ALQUIST. Why, of course; I am telling you. Go, prepare everything. See to it. Or must I call others to take her in?

PRIMUS. [*Seizes a heavy pestle*] If you do that I will kill you.

ALQUIST. [*Laughing*] Kill me! Kill me! What will the Robots do then?

PRIMUS. [*Throwing himself on his knees*] Sir, take me. I am made the same as she is, from the same material, on the same day. Take my life, sir. [*Undoing jacket*] Cut here, here!

ALQUIST. Go! I wish to cut Helena. Do it quickly.

PRIMUS. Take me instead of her. I will not shriek, I will not cry out. Take my life——

ALQUIST. Do you not wish to live, then?

PRIMUS. Not without her. I will not without her. You must not kill Helena.

ALQUIST. [*Touching his head gently*] H'm, I don't know. Listen—consider the matter. It is hard to die. It is better to live.

PRIMUS. [*Standing up*] Sir, do not be afraid to cut. I am stronger than she is.

ALQUIST. [*Ringing a bell*] Ah, Primus, it is a long time since I was a young man. Do not be afraid, nothing shall happen to Helena.

PRIMUS. [*Fastening his jacket*] I am going, sir.

ALQUIST. Wait!

Enter HELENA

Come here, girl; show yourself to me. So you are Helena? [*Smoothing her hair*] Do not be afraid, do not wince. Do you remember Mrs. Domain? Ah, Helena, what hair she had! Will you help me? I will dissect Primus.

HELENA. [*Uttering a scream*] Primus?

ALQUIST. Yes, yes, it must be done, you see. I really wanted—yes, I wanted to cut you. But Primus has offered himself instead.

HELENA. [*Covering her face*] Primus?

ALQUIST. Certainly. What of it? Ah, child, you can weep. Tell me, what is Primus to you?

PRIMUS. Do not torment her, sir.

ALQUIST. Quiet, Primus, quiet. Why do you weep? Heavens! supposing Primus is no more. You will forget him in a week. Go and think yourself lucky to be alive.

HELENA. [*Softly*] I am ready.

ALQUIST. Ready?

HELENA. For you to cut me.

ALQUIST. You? You are beautiful, Helena. It would be a pity.

HELENA. I am ready.

    [PRIMUS *goes to protect her*]

Let me be, Primus.

PRIMUS. He shall not touch you, Helena. [*Holding her*] [*To* ALQUIST] Old man, you shall kill neither of us.

ALQUIST. Why?

PRIMUS. We—we—belong to one another.

ALQUIST. Now you have said it. [*Opens the door,* C.]—Go!

PRIMUS. Where?

ALQUIST. Wherever you like. Helena, lead him. Go, Adam—Go, Eve. You shall be his wife. Be her husband, Primus.   [*Exeunt* PRIMUS *and* HELENA [*He closes the door behind them*] [*Alone*] Oh, blessed day. Oh, festival of the sixth day! [*Sits down at the desk, throws the books on the ground. Then he opens a Bible, turns over the pages and reads*] 'And God created man in His own image; in the image of God created He him, male and female created He them. And God blessed them and said: Be fruitful and multiply and replenish the earth, and subdue it, and hold sway over the fishes of the sea and the fowls of the air, and over all living creatures which move upon the earth.' [*Standing up*] 'And God saw what He had made, and it was good. And the evening and morning were the sixth day.'

[HELENA *and* PRIMUS *pass by garlanded*]

'Now, Lord, lettest Thou Thy servant depart in peace, according to Thy will, for mine eyes have seen Thy salvation.'

[*Standing up—stretching out his hands*]

CURTAIN

THE
INSECT PLAY

('And so *ad infinitum*')

*An Entomological Review
in three acts, a Prologue and
an Epilogue*

by

THE BROTHERS ČAPEK

Translated from the Czech by Paul Selver and adapted for
the English Stage by Nigel Playfair and
Clifford Bax

So, Naturalists observe, a flea
Has smaller fleas that on him prey;
And these have smaller still to bite 'em,
And so proceed *ad infinitum*.
                              DEAN SWIFT

'And so *ad infinitum*' was first produced at the Regent
Theatre, on 5 May 1923.

SCENES

DRAMATIS PERSONAE

(In the order of their appearance)

A TRAMP
A LEPIDOPTERIST
CLYTIE ⎫
OTTO   ⎪
FELIX   ⎬ *Butterflies*
IRIS   ⎪
VICTOR ⎭
A CHRYSALIS
MR. BEETLE
MRS. BEETLE
ANOTHER BEETLE
ICHNEUMON FLY
HIS DAUGHTER
MR. CRICKET
MRS. CRICKET
A PARASITE
OTHER CREEPERS AND CRAWLERS
THE BLIND TIMEKEEPER   ⎫
THE CHIEF ENGINEER   ⎪
THE SECOND ENGINEER   ⎪
AN INVENTOR   ⎪
A MESSENGER   ⎬ *Ants*
A SIGNAL OFFICER   ⎪
A JOURNALIST   ⎪
A PHILANTHROPIST   ⎪
THE COMMANDER-IN-CHIEF OF THE YELLOWS, &C. ⎭
FIRST   ⎫
SECOND ⎬ *Moths*
THIRD   ⎭
FIRST SNAIL
SECOND SNAIL
A WOODCUTTER
A WOMAN
SCHOOL CHILDREN

PROLOGUE

THE TRAMP *is discovered, stretched out in sleep; a bottle at his side.* BUTTERFLIES *flutter across the scene.*

Enter a LEPIDOPTERIST *with a net*

LEPIDOPTERIST. There they go, there they go! Fine specimens! *Apatura Iris—Apatura Clythia*—light-blue butterflies and the Painted Lady. Wait a minute— I'll get you! That's just it—they won't wait, the silly creatures. Off again . . . Hullo—somebody here. They're settling on him. Now! Carefully. Slowly. Tiptoe! One, two, three!

> [*A butterfly settles on the tip of the* TRAMP'S *nose. The* LEPIDOPTERIST *makes a dab with his net*]

TRAMP. 'Ullo! What yer doin'? Ketchin' butterflies?

LEPIDOPTERIST. Don't move! Careful now! They're settling again. Funny creatures—they'll settle on mud, on any sort of garbage, and now they're settling on you.

TRAMP. Let 'em go. They're 'appy.

LEPIDOPTERIST. Idiot! I've lost them, confound you! There they go, there they go!

TRAMP. It's a shime—it is, reely.

> [*The* LEPIDOPTERIST *rushes out,* R. *The* TRAMP *stretches his arms, takes a pull at the emptied bottle, yawns, staggers to his feet and drops down again*]

[*Speaking to the audience*] All right—all right! Don't you worry. I 'aven't 'urt myself! I know what you think— you think I'm screwed—some of you! Rotten observa- tion—low visibility—that's what you're suffering from. You didn't catch me staggering, did you? I fell like a tree—like a hero! I was rehearsing, that's what I was doing—the fall of man! The fall of man! There's a picture for yer! Ah, you little flowers—*you* didn't think I was drunk, did you? You've too much respect for me! I'm a man, that's what I am—a lord of creation! A great thing to be, I tell yer! 'Now then, pass along there, my man!' That's what they say to me. It's wonderful! 'Clear up that rubbish heap, my man, and I'll give you a tanner, my man.' It's a fine thing to be a man. [*He succeeds in getting his balance.*]

Enter the LEPIDOPTERIST, R.

LEPIDOPTERIST. Two,—splendid Nymphalidae!

TRAMP. No offence, mister, but why'jer catch them when they're all so 'appy playing?

LEPIDOPTERIST. Playing, you call it. I'm afraid you haven't the scientific mind, my friend. It's the overture to the natural system by which Nature keeps up the balance of the population—that's what you call 'playing'. The male pursues the female; the female allures, avoids—selects—the eternal round of sex!

TRAMP. What will you do with them when you catch them?

LEPIDOPTERIST. What shall I do? Well, each insect must be identified, recorded and assigned a place in my collection. The butterfly must be carefully killed, and then carefully pinned, and properly dried, and care must be taken that the powder is not rubbed off. And it must be protected against dust and draught. A little cyanide of potassium.

TRAMP. And what's it all for?

LEPIDOPTERIST. Love of nature—if you loved nature as much as I did, my man—Careful—didn't I tell you—

they're off again. Never mind, I'll get you, see if I
don't.   [*Exit*

TRAMP. 'E's clever, that there bloke. And as for me,
P'raps I am screwed; but if I *am*, 'oo cares?
That ain't the only reason why I see
Everythink double, everythink in pairs.

Them little birds up there ... I see yer plain!
Tweet-weety-weet ... Lord! 'ow they bill and coo,
As yer might say. Them butterflies again,
What sport they 'ave—'ow prettily they woo!

Love's what they want. Some day they'll get it,
        p'raps:
Everythink does—or mostways everythink ...
(S'pose *you'd* a girl who loved all kinds of chaps—
Wouldn't *you* damn yerself, and take to drink?)

Well, 'ere's the world, and though I'm down and out,
It's worth while learnin' what it's all about.

ACT I

THE BUTTERFLIES

A hill. Many flowers and bright-coloured cushions. In the C. *a small table or bar, with high seats and coloured glass containing cold drinks and straws.*

TRAMP. I say—I say! It's a bit of all right. What price the 'Eath now? Paradise—that's what it is—Paradise! And don't it smell nice! Odi Colone, not 'alf.
[CLYTIE *runs in laughing, followed by* OTTO]

OTTO. I love you, Clytie.   [*Exeunt*

TRAMP. Butterflies! That's what they are. Butterflies, playin'. I'd like to stay 'ere and watch 'em if I wasn't so—Never mind; they can kick me out if they like. I'll lie down 'ere, comfortable.—'Pon my soul, I will. [*He takes and arranges the cushions*] [*Sleepily*] All right—that's what it is; all right.

Enter FELIX—*a poet butterfly*

FELIX. [*Ecstatically*] Iris! Iris! Where are you, Iris? If only I could find a rhyme for you!
                    All I desire is
                    Beautiful Iris . . .
No, that's wretched commonplace.
          The star to whom my thoughts aspire is
          Iris, Iris, radiant Iris.
That's no better. I know! She will reject my passion and I shall then produce an exquisite lament. For instance,—
          If only thou wert ill, hard-hearted Iris!
          Then I could melt thee with my kind inquiries . . .
                    [*Laughter behind*

112

Listen! Iris! [*He stands at the side, burying his face in his hands.*]

    [IRIS *enters, followed by* VICTOR]

IRIS. All alone, Felix? And so picturesquely mournful?

FELIX. You, Iris? I didn't think——

IRIS. Why aren't you over there? So many pretty little flappers——

FELIX. You know very well, Iris—they don't interest me.

IRIS. Poor little fellow—why not?

VICTOR [*a lady-killer*]. You mean, they don't interest you *yet*!

FELIX. They interest me no longer.

IRIS. Do you hear that, Victor? That's a nice thing to say to my face. Come here, you rude little man. Sit down close to me . . . No,—close. You don't call that close, do you? Tell me, my precious, don't women really interest you any longer?

FELIX. No—I'm weary of them.

IRIS. [*With a sigh*] Oh, you men—you're such cynics. You have your fun—as much fun as you can get—and then you say [*imitating*] 'I'm weary of them.' It's a terrible thing to be a woman.

VICTOR. Why?

IRIS. *We* never grow tired of love. Have you had a terrible past, Felix? When did you first fall in love?

FELIX. I don't know. I forget. It was so long ago. I was a schoolboy.

VICTOR. Ah, you were still a caterpillar. Gobbling up all the leaves.

IRIS. A little kitty kitty kitty caterpillar. Was she dark and beautiful?

FELIX. As beautiful——

IRIS. As what?

FELIX. As beautiful as you,

IRIS. And did she love you?

FELIX. I don't know. I never spoke to her.

IRIS. Good heavens! What did you do to her then?

FELIX. I looked at her from afar.

VICTOR. Sitting on a green leaf?

FELIX. And wrote poems, letters—my first novel.

VICTOR. It's appalling the number of leaves a caterpillar uses up.

IRIS. Don't be nasty, Victor. Look, his eyes are full of tears.

VICTOR. Tears? Poor little cry-baby.

FELIX. They're not, they're not!

IRIS. Let me see—look into my eyes quickly.

VICTOR. One, two, three, four—Ah! I knew he couldn't hold out any longer.

IRIS. What's the colour of *my* eyes, Felix dear?

FELIX. Blue—like Heaven.

IRIS. Yours are brown—golden-brown. I don't care for blue eyes, they're so cold. Poor Clytie has green eyes, hasn't she? Do you like Clytie's eyes, Felix?

FELIX. Clytie's? I don't know. Yes—she has beautiful eyes.

114

IRIS. Oh, but her legs are dreadfully thick! You're such bad judges of women, you poets.

VICTOR. Have you read the last poem that Felix published? It came out in the Spring Anthology.

IRIS. Read it me, quickly.

FELIX. No, no, I won't let you read it to her. It's bad— it's old—I've passed that stage long ago.

VICTOR. It's called 'The Eternal Life'.

FELIX. You're not to read it—really!

VICTOR. [*Reads*]
> There's nothing true. The earth and sky
>   Were false when first created;
> And you and I will surely lie
>   When love is consummated.

IRIS. That's witty, isn't it, Victor? How did you think of it? What's consummated, Felix?

VICTOR. From the Latin 'consummare'. It means that Love has—ahem—achieved its aim.

IRIS. What aim?

VICTOR. Well—the usual one.

IRIS. Oh, how shocking, Felix. I'm afraid of you. Is Latin always so immoral?

FELIX. Don't, Iris. It's such a bad poem.

IRIS. Why, bad?

FELIX. There's no real passion in it.

IRIS. Victor, you will find my fan in the garden.

VICTOR. Oh, don't let *me* disturb you,   [*Exit*

IRIS. Quick, Felix—tell me the truth. You can tell me everything.

FELIX. Iris, Iris—how can you bear him? That fop, that silk-hatted satyr!

IRIS. Victor?

FELIX. How foully he thinks of love, of you, of everything.

IRIS. Poor Victor—he's so soothing. No, Felix, talk about poetry. I'm fond of poetry . . .
           'Were false when first created'
Felix, you're frightfully clever . . .
           'When love is consummated'
Tell me, Felix, poets are dreadfully, hideously, passionate, aren't they?

FELIX. Oh, Iris, I've grown out of what's in that poem a long time.

IRIS. If only that Latin word wasn't so coarse. I can stand anything, anything, but it mustn't have a horrid name. Felix, you must be tender and delicate with women. If I were to let you kiss me, you wouldn't give me a horrid name, would you?

FELIX. Iris, I wouldn't dare to kiss you.

IRIS. Be brave, little boy. Faint heart never won—Tell me, whom did you write that poem to? To Clytie?

FELIX. No, no, no

IRIS. To whom, then?

FELIX. To nobody, upon my honour, to nobody; or rather, to all the women in the world.

IRIS. Good gracious! All the women in the—— Felix,

you're a terrible rake. But you *must* let me know one thing—who's your [*whispering*] ladybird now?

FELIX. You won't tell any one—you really won't?

IRIS. No.

FELIX. I haven't got one.

IRIS. What?

FELIX. Not yet—I swear it. [*Very simply.*]

IRIS. Oh what a naughty fib! How many women have you told the tale to? I see through you, Felix. You're a dangerous man.

FELIX. Iris, dear, don't laugh at me. I've had awful experiences—in my imagination. Terrible disappointments. Love-affairs without number—but only in my dreams. Dreams are the poet's life. I know all women, and I've not known one—I swear it, Iris.

IRIS. Then why do you say you are tired of women?

FELIX. Oh, Iris, every one disparages the thing that he loves best.

IRIS. Do you mean dark women? You love Clytie—the cat.

FELIX. No—dreams, eternal dreams.

IRIS. You have such passionate eyes, Felix. You're awfully clever. What are you thinking about now?

FELIX. About you. Woman is a riddle.

IRIS. Guess it then. But not too roughly, please.

FELIX. I cannot see into the depths of your eyes.

IRIS. [*Crossly*] Oh, then look somewhere else.

FELIX. Iris, I——

IRIS. I'm in a queer mood today. How stupid it is to be a woman. I should like to be a man—to kiss, to tempt, to overcome. Oh, Felix, I should make such a fearfully passionate man. I should—I should seize everything I wanted, brutally, savagely. What a pity you aren't a girl. Let's pretend, shall we? You be Iris, and I'll be your Felix.

FELIX. No, Iris—it's too dangerous to be Felix. I couldn't let you. It means desiring something, desiring something——

IRIS. [*In a whisper*] Oh, Felix, not something—everything!

FELIX. There is something greater than desiring everything.

IRIS. Is there? What is it?

FELIX. Desiring the impossible.

IRIS. [*Coldly and crossly*] Oh, of course, you're perfectly ·right. You're always right—so right. What can be keeping Victor so long? Would you mind calling him?

FELIX. Iris, I haven't offended you? I haven't said too much?

IRIS. No—I shouldn't call it too much!

FELIX. To desire the unattainable. Iris, I was mad to talk to you like that.

IRIS. Or at least impolite. Really, you know, you're rather crude, my little man. When you're in the company of ladies, you shouldn't behave as if you were longing for something that isn't there.

FELIX. The unattainable *is* there.

IRIS. [*Looking round from her mirror*] Where?

FELIX. Your image, Iris,

IRIS. My image? Have you fallen in love with my image? Look, my image has heard you. Kiss it quickly.

FELIX. It is as unapproachable as you.

IRIS. Am I unapproachable? How do you know?

FELIX. If I didn't know that, I shouldn't love you.

IRIS. But must one always be unapproachable?

FELIX. There is no true love except in the unapproachable.

IRIS. Do you think so? What about
          'shall surely lie
       When love is'——
you know!

FELIX. Don't, Iris—not again.

IRIS. Make a poem for me, quickly. Something passionate.

FELIX. Now that at last we have met,
     Think you I care what may follow?
  Let me be snared in a net,
     Let me be snapped by a swallow——

  I shall have tasted of bliss,
     I shall have flown where the fire is.
  Ah, could we die in a kiss,
     Beautiful exquisite Iris!

IRIS. How perfect!

CLYTIE. [*Outside*] Iris! Iris!

IRIS. That tiresome Clytie—with that awful hanger-on of hers—just as we——

Enter CLYTIE

CLYTIE. Fancy, Iris—Otto says—Oh, you've got Felix

E   *119*

here. How are you, Felix? Iris, you've been teasing him—he's blushing.

Enter OTTO

OTTO. Got you now, Clytie—Oh, I beg your pardon. How do you do, Iris? How are you, my boy?

[FELIX *sits down, sighing*

IRIS. You're out of breath, Clytie.

CLYTIE. Otto has been chasing me.

OTTO. She flew away, so I *had* to follow her.

Enter VICTOR

VICTOR. Quite a little party.

CLYTIE. [*Drinking*] Oh, I'm so thirsty.

IRIS. Take care of yourself, dearest. Victor, see how thin she's become again. You're looking terrible—you really are.

CLYTIE. Thank you, darling. You will be a mother to me, won't you?

VICTOR. Were you at the Garden Party yesterday?

CLYTIE. Yesterday? Pooh—that's ancient history.

VICTOR. Marvellous weather.

IRIS. [*To* CLYTIE] Just a moment, dearest. What have you been doing? Your bodice is torn.

CLYTIE. Thank you, darling—Felix! You look so sad. What's the matter with you, my precious?

FELIX. I'm thinking.

CLYTIE. Thinking? What do you keep thinking about?

FELIX. Men's minds were given them to use.

CLYTIE. And women's?

FELIX. To misuse.

IRIS. Oh, isn't that good, Felix!

CLYTIE: The nasty little fellow hates me.

VICTOR. Be careful, Clytie—that's the first step towards love.

OTTO. Eh, what's that?

IRIS. Felix and love? The idea! Why, he wrote something about women—wait ....

FELIX. Iris, how can you! Don't!

IRIS.   There's nothing true. The earth and sky
              Were false when first created;
          And you and I will surely lie
              When love is consummated.

CLYTIE. Will surely what?

IRIS. 'Surely lie', dearest.

VICTOR. Felix, you scoundrel—how many women have you lied to?

OTTO. 'And you and I will surely lie'—I see! Of course! ha, ha—very good.

IRIS.   'When love is consummated.'

CLYTIE. Wait—Otto's going to laugh again.

[*He does so*

IRIS. Felix is awfully clever. None of you could find a rhyme for 'Iris'.

CLYTIE. On, couldn't we!
              Some times Iris,
              A wicked liar is.

FELIX. Oh, stop it, stop it!

OTTO. Ha, ha! That's splendid. Iris—liar is.

IRIS. Darling, you have such strange ideas about poetry. But you'll never guess what a beautiful rhyme Felix made to my name. Guess.

VICTOR. Give it up.

CLYTIE. You must tell us.

IRIS. [*Triumphantly*] 'Fire is!'

VICTOR. What?

IRIS. 'I shall have flown where the fire is!'

OTTO. Ha, ha, ha! 'Fire is'—that's jolly clever.

IRIS. Oh, you're horrid. You've no sense of art or poetry, or anything. I've no patience with you.

VICTOR. The rhymes of our little friend Felix
Are sweet as the honey a bee licks.

IRIS. Splendid, Victor. You're frightfully witty.

CLYTIE. Heavens, Victor's managed to produce a rhyme.

OTTO. 'Felix—bee licks'—that's good, damn good.

VICTOR. Poetry—what is it but lying and fooling?

IRIS. Oh no, it stirs the feelings. I'm fearfully fond of it.

OTTO. Ha! Blotto!

CLYTIE. Who's blotto?

OTTO. Rhymes with Otto. Good—eh, what?

IRIS. You're terribly clever, Otto.

OTTO. Lovely star!

IRIS. Where? What do you mean?

OTTO. That's the beginning of a poem.

CLYTIE. [*Yawning*] Oh, do stop talking this literary stuff. I'm fed up with it.

VICTOR. [*Aside to* IRIS] Not so much as I'm fed up with her!

IRIS. *Are* you? Are you really, Victor? I feel like kissing you. Catch me—catch me if you can.

[*She runs off, and* VICTOR *after her*]

CLYTIE. What a fright! What a figure!—Felix!

FELIX. Yes?

CLYTIE. How ever could you fall in love with her?

FELIX. With whom?

CLYTIE. With that dowdy thing!

FELIX. Whom do you mean?

CLYTIE. Iris, of course.

FELIX. I? What can you be thinking of? That was over—long ago.

CLYTIE. I understand. Iris is so awfully ignorant—and such thick ankles. Oh, Felix, at your age we have so many illusions about women.

FELIX. I haven't, Clytie. I passed that stage when I was a boy.

CLYTIE. No, Felix, you don't know women. Sit here beside me—no, closer. You've no idea what they're like —their minds, their souls, their bodies. You're so young.

FELIX. Oh, if I were! I've had so much experience.

CLYTIE. You *must* be young—it's the fashion. To be young, a butterfly, and a poet—Is there anything more beautiful in the world?

FELIX. It is not beautiful; it is an agony. The fate of the young is to suffer, and a poet to suffer a hundredfold.

CLYTIE. It's the fate of a poet to be terribly happy. Ah, Felix, you remind me of my first love.

FELIX. Who was he?

CLYTIE. Nobody—I forget. None of my lovers was the first. Ah, that Victor! I *hate* men. Let's be friends, Felix—like two girls together.

FELIX. Like two girls?

CLYTIE. Love's nothing to you. Love's so common I want something special, something pure, something new.

FELIX. A poem.

CLYTIE. [*Doubtfully*] Yes, that'll do—You see how much I like you.

FELIX. Listen!

> She came in the blue Spring weather,
>   Gay as a foxglove is;
> And our two hearts rhymed together,
>   And our lips were one in a kiss.

CLYTIE. What's that?

FELIX. A poem—the beginning.

CLYTIE. And how does it go on?

FELIX. I'll bring you the end in a minute. But I outgrow my work so quickly than when I reach the end I may have to alter the beginning.

CLYTIE. [*In disgust*] Bah! [*To* OTTO] Now then, can't you leave your moustache alone?

OTTO. Love me, Clytie.

CLYTIE. Visitors are requested not to touch.

OTTO. Love me, Clytie.

CLYTIE. Otto, you're so irresistibly handsome.

OTTO. I love *you* madly.

CLYTIE. I know—I know. Say 'ninety-nine'.

OTTO. Ninety-nine.

CLYTIE. Say it again.

OTTO. Ninety-nine.

CLYTIE. How it rumbles in your chest—like thunder. Otto, you're fearfully strong, aren't you?

OTTO. Cly-Cly-Cly——

CLYTIE. What's the matter now?

OTTO. Love me, Clytie.

CLYTIE. Oh, don't be tiresome.

OTTO. Love me, love me now!

CLYTIE. [*Flying off*] Wait, wait, wait—don't be impatient.

OTTO. [*After her*] Love me, Clytie!   [*Exeunt*

TRAMP. There now—that poor male insec'! Well, I'm blest——
Goin' 'alf balmy for them flighty things! . . .
As fer that kind of female—why, she's jest
A man-trap 'idden be'ind two silky wings.
    [CLYTIE *flying in from the other side, and powdering herself at the mirror*]

CLYTIE. Whew! Just managed to get away from him, only just!

TRAMP. Ho! 'Igh Society, what? Powder yer nose,
Strip to yer waist—and let the *rest* show through!
Put it blunt-like—Lord Alf and Lady Rose
Be'ave exactly like them insec's do.

CLYTIE. Are you a butterfly?
   [TRAMP *throws his cap at her as if to catch her*]
Aren't you a butterfly?

TRAMP. I'm a man.

CLYTIE. What's that? Is it alive?

TRAMP. Well, in a manner o' speakin', lady.

CLYTIE. [*Flying up to him*] Can it love?

TRAMP. Oh yus. Reg'lar butterfly.

CLYTIE. How thrilling you are! Why do you have black down on your face? And—oh, it pricks!

TRAMP. Down! That's scrub. 'Aven't shaved for a fortnight, I 'aven't.

CLYTIE. There's a fragrance in the air about you.

TRAMP. Stale baccy—that's what it is.

CLYTIE. So delicious—so new!

TRAMP. [*Throwing cap again*] Shoo, yer 'ussy!

CLYTIE. [*Flying away*] Chase me, chase me!

TRAMP. Oh, you baggage, you.

CLYTIE. [*Approaching*] Let me come near you. You are so unusual.

TRAMP. I've met the likes of you afore, I 'ave. [*Catches her hand*] I've 'eld 'er 'ands like this, and told 'er if she'd

smile at me I'd let 'er go—and then I let 'er go. Better
for me and better for 'er, if I'd killed 'er straight off.
[*Lets her go*] 'Ere, sling yer 'ook. I don't want yer.

CLYTIE. [*Flying away to mirror*] How strange you are!

TRAMP. Oh, yer strumpet, you, yer painted 'arlot!

CLYTIE. [*To him again*] Say it again, say it again, so
strange, so coarse—I—·

TRAMP. Garn—yer white-faced 'arridan! Isn't that
enough for yer?

CLYTIE. I love you, I love you!

TRAMP. Go—get a move on. I 'ate the sight of yer.

CLYTIE. Oh, you wretch! [*She returns to the mirror.*]

IRIS. [*Running, out of breath*] Something to drink—quick!

CLYTIE. Where have you been?

IRIS. On the hill-tops—it was so hot.

CLYTIE. Where did you leave Victor?

IRIS. Victor? Who's Victor?

CLYTIE. Why, you went off with him.

IRIS. Oh yes, of course—but that was only fun. I remember now. Something awfully funny happened. It'll
make you scream. He kept running after me ... ha,
ha, ha.

CLYTIE. Why did you leave him?

IRIS. I'm telling you. He kept running after me, and
suddenly—ha, ha, ha. A bird flew along and ate him up!

CLYTIE. You don't say!

IRIS. As true as I'm standing here. I thought I should

have died. [*She bursts into laughter and buries her head in the cushions.*]

CLYTIE. What *is* the matter with you?

IRIS. Oh, those men!

CLYTIE. Do you mean Victor?

IRIS. No—Otto. Victor was eaten by a bird. Just fancy—immediately after, up came your Otto. Oh, the look in his eyes—all on fire—and then—ha, ha, ha!

CLYTIE. What then?

IRIS. He came after me. 'Love me, Iris,' he said, 'love me, love me.'

CLYTIE. Well, did you?

IRIS. Ha, ha! Guess again. 'Love me, Iris, love me!'

FELIX. [*Flying in with a pen in his hand*] Here it is, Clytie, listen!

> She came in the light Spring weather,
> Gay as a jonquil is——
>
> [*Iris laughs hysterically*

What's the matter?

IRIS. What a vulgar fellow! I could have strangled him.

CLYTIE. Otto?

FELIX. Listen, Clytie——
> And our two hearts rhymed together
> And our lips were one in a kiss.
> She said, 'How strange to discover
> The lessons a kiss can teach!
> You have turned a child to a lover
> As a peach-flower turns to a peach.'

IRIS. Is my hair horribly untidy?

CLYTIE. Horribly. Let me, darling—Beast!

IRIS. You're angry, aren't you? [*Imitating*] Otto loves wonderfully.

Enter OTTO

OTTO. I love you, Iris

IRIS. Catch me if you can.   [*Exit*

OTTO. I love *you*, Clytie.

CLYTIE. Follow me, follow me.   [*Exeunt*

FELIX. Wait, wait!

TRAMP. Fool!

FELIX. Who's that? Somebody, anyway I'll read *you* the end.

> I answered 'But each new-comer
> Is only supreme for an hour . . .'

TRAMP. [*Striking at him with his cap*] Shoo!

FELIX. [*Flying about*]

> I answered 'But each new-comer
> Is only supreme for an hour.
> The fruit may fall with the summer
> But Spring will renew the flower.'

ALL THE BUTTERFLIES *enter fluttering*

TRAMP. Butterflies! Nice *birds* them butterflies!

CURTAIN

ACT II

CREEPERS AND CRAWLERS

SCENE: *A sandy hillock—Various holes, etc.*

BEETLES *are quarrelling over a* CHRYSALIS, *which is seized first by one then the other*

CHRYSALIS. The whole world is bursting into blossom. I am being born.

TRAMP. [*Raising his head—he is lying half asleep*] How much?

CHRYSALIS. The Great Adventure begins.

TRAMP. Right oh! [*Settles down again.*]

[*Pause*

MR. BEETLE. [*Behind the scenes*] What yer getting at?

MRS. BEETLE. [*Behind the scenes*] Me?

MR. BEETLE. Yes, you—you lump of rubbish.

MRS. BEETLE. Silly swine.

MR. BEETLE. Fathead.

MRS. BEETLE. Fathead yourself—mind where you're going.

They enter, rolling a huge ball of dirt

MR. BEETLE. It's all right, isn't it?

MRS. BEETLE. I'm all of a tremble.

MR. BEETLE. Our capital—that's what it is—our lovely capital—careful—careful.

MRS. BEETLE. Can't be too careful with our capital— our little pile.

MR. BEETLE. How we've saved and scraped and toiled and moiled to come by it.

MRS. BEETLE. Night and morning, toiled and moiled and saved and scraped.

MR. BEETLE. And we've seen it grow and grow, haven't we, bit by bit—our little ball of blessedness.

MRS. BEETLE. Our very own it is.

MR. BEETLE. Our very own.

MRS. BEETLE. Our life's work.

MR. BEETLE. Smell it, old woman—pinch it—feel the weight of it. Ours—ours.

MRS. BEETLE. A godsend.

MR. BEETLE. A blessing—straight from Heaven—capital —capital.

CHRYSALIS. Eternal night is breaking:
          The universe is waking:
          One minute, just one minute
          And I—*I*—shall be in it.

MRS. BEETLE. Husband.

MR. BEETLE. What is it, old woman?

MRS. BEETLE. Ha, ha, ha!

MR. BEETLE. Ha, ha, ha! Wife!

MRS. BEETLE. What is it, old man?

MR. BEETLE. Ha, ha! It's fine to own something— property—the dream of your life, the fruit of your labours.

MRS. BEETLE. Ha, ha, ha!

MR. BEETLE. I'm off my head with joy—I'm going balmy.

MRS. BEETLE. Why?

MR. BEETLE. With worry. Now we've got our little pile that we've so looked forward to, we've got to work and work and work to make another one.

MRS. BEETLE. Why another one?

MR. BEETLE. Silly—so that we can have two, of course,

MRS. BEETLE. Two? Quite right—quite right—two.

MR. BEETLE. Just fancy—two—at least two, say three. Every one who's made his pile has to make another.

MRS. BEETLE. So that he can have two?

MR. BEETLE. Yes, or three.

MRS. BEETLE. Husband.

MR. BEETLE. Well, what is it?

MRS. BEETLE. I'm scared—S'posin' some one was to steal it from us.

MR. BEETLE. What?

MRS. BEETLE. Our capital—our little pile—our all in all.

MR. BEETLE. Our pi-ile—My gawd—don't frighten me.

MRS. BEETLE. We oughtn't to roll it about with us till we've made another one, dearie, did we?

MR. BEETLE. I'll tell you what—we'll invest it—In—vest it—store it up—bury it. That's what we'll do—nice and deep—nice and deep.

MRS. BEETLE. I hope nobody finds it.

MR. BEETLE. Eh, what's that? Finds it—·No, of course they won't. Our little bit of capital.

MRS. BEETLE. Our nest-egg—Oh, bless me—I hope no one does—our little all.

MR. BEETLE. Wait—stay here and watch it—Watch it careful—don't let your eyes off it, not for a minute—Capital—Capital.

MRS. BEETLE. Where yer off to?

MR. BEETLE. To look for a hole—a little hole—a deep hole—deep and narrer to bury it in—out of harm's way—Careful—Careful.   [*Exit*

MRS. BEETLE. Husband—husband, come back—wait a bit—I've found one—such a nice hole—Husband! He's gone! If I could only look into it—No, I mustn't leave yer. But only a peep—Here, stay here good and quiet, darling. Hubby'll be back soon—in half a jiff, half a jiff—So long, keep good—half a ji——

Enters the lair of the ICHNEUMON FLY

CHRYSALIS. Oh, to be born—to be born—into the great new world.

Enter a STRANGE BEETLE

STRANGE BEETLE. They've gone—now's my chance. [*Rolls pile away.*]

TRAMP. 'Ere, mind where yer going to.

STRANGE BEETLE. Mind yer feet.

TRAMP. What's that yer rolling?

STRANGE BEETLE. Ha, ha! That's my capital—my little pile, my all.

TRAMP. Bit niffy, ain't it?

STRANGE BEETLE. Eh?

TRAMP. It smells.

STRANGE BEETLE. Capital don't smell—Off you go, my precious—This way, my little all, my nest-egg, my capital.   [*Exit*

MRS. BEETLE. Oh dear, oh dear. That's somebody's house, that is—We can't put you there, my jewel. Oh, where's it gone to? Where's it gone to? My little pile— where's it gone to?

TRAMP. Why, not 'arf a minute——

MRS. BEETLE. [*Rushing at him*] Thief—thief—What 'ave you done with my pile?

TRAMP. I'm telling yer.

MRS. BEETLE. Here, give it back—yer wretch.

TRAMP. Just this minute a gentleman rolled it away over there.

MRS. BEETLE. What gentleman? Who?

TRAMP. A pot-bellied fellow, a fat, round chap.

MRS. BEETLE. My husband?

TRAMP. A feller with an ugly mug and crooked feet.

MRS. BEETLE. That's my husband.

TRAMP. His capital he said it was.

MRS. BEETLE. That's him—he must have found a hole— Husband—My precious—Darling! Where is the blasted fool?

TRAMP. That's where he rolled it to.

MRS. BEETLE. Coo-eh! Couldn't he have called me? Husband, my precious! I'll learn yer—Our capital— our all—our little pile.   [*Exit*

TRAMP.   Them butterflies was gay
           And foolish, yer might say:
           But these 'ere beetles—lumme,
           They *do* work, anyway!

> So, 'ere's to wish 'em luck——
> Though gatherin' balls of muck
> Is jest about as rummy
> As anythink I've struck.

CHRYSALIS. O universe, prepare! O space, expand!
The mightiest of all happenings is at hand.

TRAMP. What's that?

CHRYSALIS. I'm being born.

TRAMP. That's good—and what are you going to be?

CHRYSALIS. I don't know—I don't know—Something
great.

TRAMP. Ah, ha!

CHRYSALIS. I'll do something extraordinary—I'm being
born.

TRAMP. What *you* want's life, my son.

CHRYSALIS. When half a minute's gone,
       Something immense, unbounded,
Will happen here.
TRAMP.   Go on!

CHRYSALIS. I shall do something great!

TRAMP. What?

CHRYSALIS. When I change my state,
       The world will be astounded!

TRAMP. Well—'urry up. I'll wait.
       Enter ICHNEUMON FLY, *dragging the corpse of a*
             CRICKET *to its lair*

ICHNEUMON FLY. Look, larva, daddy's bringing you
something nice.
            Enters his lair

CHRYSALIS. [*Shouting*]
>The torment of my birth
>Is tearing the whole earth.
>She groans to set me free——

TRAMP. Then get a move on. See?

ICHNEUMON FLY. [*Returning*] No, no, daughter, you must eat. You mustn't come out—it wouldn't do at all. Daddy'll soon be back and he'll bring you something nice. What would you like, piggywiggy?

Enter LARVA

LARVA. Daddy, I'm bored here.

ICHNEUMON FLY. Ha, ha! That's a nice thing to say. Give daddy a kiss—Daddy'll bring you something tasty. Would you like a follow of cricket? Ha, ha—not a bad idea.

LARVA. I'd like—I don't know what I'd like.

ICHNEUMON FLY. She doesn't know what she'd like, bless her little heart. I'll find something you'll like— Ta-ta! Daddy must go to work now—Daddy must go a hunting and fetch something for his popsy-wopsy. Ta-ta! Go back now, poppet, and wait for your din-din. Ta-ta! [*Exit* LARVA

ICHNEUMON FLY. [*To Tramp*] Who are you?

TRAMP. I?

ICHNEUMON FLY. Are you edible?

TRAMP. Yes, I don't think.

ICHNEUMON FLY. [*Sniffing*] No—not fresh enough—Who are you?

TRAMP. Oh, any sort of skunk, I am.

ICHNEUMON FLY. [*Bowing*] Pleased to meet you. Any family?

TRAMP. Not as I am aware of.

ICHNEUMON FLY. Did you see her?

TRAMP. 'Er? Who?

ICHNEUMON FLY. My Larva. Charming, eh? Smart child—And how she grows, and what a twist she's got. Children are a great joy, aren't they?

TRAMP. I've 'eard 'em well spoken of.

ICHNEUMON FLY. Well, of course they are, you take it from me—One who knows. When you have them, at least you know what you're working for. That's life, that is. Children want to grow, to eat, to laugh, to dance, to play, don't they? Am I right?

TRAMP. Children want a lot.

ICHNEUMON FLY. Would you believe it, I take her two or three crickets every day. Do you think she eats them all up? No—Only the titbits—A splendid child, eh?

TRAMP. I should say so.

ICHNEUMON FLY. I'm proud of her—real proud. Takes after me—just like her daddy, eh? Ha, ha! And here I stand gossiping, when I ought to be at work. Oh, the fuss and the running about—Up early, home late, but as long as you're doing it for some one worth doing it for, what does it matter? Am I right?

TRAMP. I suppose you are.

ICHNEUMON FLY. A pity you aren't edible, isn't it? It is, really. I must take her something, you know, mustn't I? You see that yourself, don't you? [*Fingering* CHRYSALIS.]

CHRYSALIS. I proclaim the re-birth of the world.

ICHNEUMON FLY. Ah! You aren't ripe yet—Pity.

CHRYSALIS. I shall inspire—I shall create.

ICHNEUMON FLY. It's a great responsibility to bring up children—A great worry, isn't it? Feeding the poor little mites, paying for their education and putting them out into the world. That's no trifle, I can tell you. Well, I must be off now—Au revoir—Pleased to have met you—Ta-ta, my chicken—Be good!   [*Exit*

TRAMP. This 'as me fairly beat. That fly destroys
The cricket jest to feed 'is girls and boys;
But that pore 'armless cricket found life sweet,
Same as 'e does—No! Nature 'as me beat!

LARVA. [*Crawling out of hole*] Daddy! Daddy!

TRAMP. So you're the Larva. Let's have a look at you,

LARVA. How ugly you are!

TRAMP. Am I? Why?

LARVA. I don't know—Oh, how bored I am! I want—I want——

TRAMP. What yer want?

LARVA. I don't know. Yes I do—To tear up something—Something alive—that wriggles.

TRAMP. 'Ere, what's come over yer?

LARVA. Ugly—ugly—ugly! [*Crawls away.*]

TRAMP. Where's Mr. Manners?—Blowed if I'd feed a daughter
Like 'er. Perliteness—that's what *I'd* 'ave taught 'er.

Enter MR. BEETLE

MR. BEETLE. [*Calling*] Come along, old girl. I've found a hole. Where are you? Where's my pile? Where's my wife?

TRAMP. Your wife? Do you mean that old harridan? That greasy fat bundle of rags?

MR. BEETLE. That's her—Where's my pile?

TRAMP. That old tub in petticoats?

MR. BEETLE. That's her—that's her—She had my pile— What's she done with my pile?

TRAMP. Why, your beauty went to look for you.

MR. BEETLE. Did she? Where's my pile?

TRAMP. That great ball of muck?

MR. BEETLE. Yes, yes. My nest-egg—my savings—my capital. Where's my beautiful pile? I left my wife with it.

TRAMP. Some gentleman rolled it away over there. Your wife wasn't here at the time.

MR. BEETLE. Where was she? Where is she?

TRAMP. She went after him. She thought it was you. She kept shoutin' for yer.

MR. BEETLE. I'm not asking about her. Where's my pile, I say?

TRAMP. Gentleman rolled it away.

MR. BEETLE. Rolled it away? My pile? Gawd in 'eaven! Catch him. Catch him. Thief! Murder! All my little lot. All I've saved. They've killed me, they've done me in. Who cares about my wife? It's my pile they've taken. Help—stop thief! Murder!

TRAMP. Ha, ha, ha!
       Crikee! 'E don't want pleasure
       But jest to pile up treasure;
       And when the old sly copper—
       Death—comes and nabs 'im proper,

> 'E'll still be like a nigger
> Sweatin' to make it bigger,
> Still 'eavin' and still puffin' . . .
> And what's he gained? Why, nuffin'!

MR. CRICKET. [*Off stage*] Look out, darling—take care you don't stumble. Here we are—here we are. Oopsi-daisy! This is where we live—this is our new little home. Careful—You haven't hurt yourself, have you?

Enter MR. *and* MRS. CRICKET

MRS. CRICKET. No, Cricket, don't be absurd.

MR. CRICKET. But darling, you must be careful—When you're expecting—and now open the peephole—look—How do you like it?

MRS. CRICKET. Oh, darling, how tired I am!

MR. CRICKET. Sit down, darling, sit down. My popsy must take great care of herself.

MRS. CRICKET. What a long way—And all the move! Oh, men never know half the trouble moving is.

MR. CRICKET. Oh darling, come, come—Look, darling, look.

MRS. CRICKET. Now don't get cross, you horrid man,

MR. CRICKET. I won't say another word, really I won't. Fancy, Mrs. Cricket won't take care of herself, and in her state too—What do you think of her?

MRS. CRICKET. You naughty man—how can you joke about it?

MR. CRICKET. But darling, I'm so happy. Just fancy, all the little crickets, the noise, the chirping—[*Imitates the noise and laughs.*]

MRS. CRICKET. You—you silly boy—wants to be a great big Daddy, eh?

MR. CRICKET. And don't you want to be a Mummy too? —my Popsy?

MRS. CRICKET. Yes'm does! Is this our new home?

MR. CRICKET. Our little nest. Commodious little villa residence.

MRS. CRICKET. Will it be dry? Who built it?

MR. CRICKET. Why, goodness me, another Cricket lived here years ago.

MRS. CRICKET. Fancy, and has he moved?

MR. CRICKET. Ha, ha—Yes, he's moved. Don't you know where to? Guess.

MRS. CRICKET. I don't know—What a long time you take saying anything—Do tell me, Cricket, quickly.

MR. CRICKET. Well, yesterday a bird got him—Snap, snip, snap. So we're moving into his house. By Jove, what a slice of luck!

MRS. CRICKET. Gobbled him up alive? How horrible!

MR. CRICKET. Eh? A godsend for us. I did laugh. Tralala, etc. We'll put up a plate. [*Puts up plate with 'Mr. Cricket, musician'*] Where shall we put it? More to the right? Higher?

MRS. CRICKET. And you saw him eaten?

MR. CRICKET. I'm telling you—like that—snap, snip!

MRS. CRICKET. Horrible! Cricket, I have such a queer feeling.

MR. CRICKET. Good heavens—Perhaps it's—no, it couldn't be, not yet!

MRS. CRICKET. Oh dear, I'm so frightened.

MR. CRICKET. Nothing to be frightened of, dear— Every lady——

MRS. CRICKET. It's all very well for you to talk— Cricket, will you always love me?

MR. CRICKET. Of course, darling—Dear me, don't cry— come, love.

MRS. CRICKET. Show me how he swallowed him—Snip, snap.

MR. CRICKET. Snip, snap,

MRS. CRICKET. Oh, how funny! [*Has hysterics.*]

MR. CRICKET. Well, well. There's nothing to cry about. [*Sits beside her*] We'll furnish this place beautifully. And as soon as we can run to it, we'll put up some——

MRS. CRICKET. Curtains?

MR. CRICKET. Curtains, of course! How clever of you to think of it. Give me a kiss.

MRS. CRICKET. Never mind that now—Don't be silly.

MR. CRICKET. Of course I'm silly. Guess what I've brought?

MRS. CRICKET. Curtains!

MR. CRICKET. No, something smaller—Where did I——?

MRS. CRICKET. Quick, quick, let me see.
> [MR. CRICKET *takes out a rattle*
Oh, how sweet, Cricket! Give it to me.

MR. CRICKET. [*Sings*]
> When Dr. Stork had brought their child,
>   Their teeny-weeny laddy,
> All day about the cradle smiled
>   His mumsy and his daddy:
> And 'Cricket, cricket, cricket,
>   You pretty little thing'—
> Is now the song that all day long
>   They sing, sing, sing.

MRS. CRICKET. Lend it me, darling—Oh, daddy—I'm so pleased. Rattle it.

MR. CRICKET. Darling.

MRS. CRICKET. [*Singing*] Cricket, cricket, cricket!

MR. CRICKET. Now I must run round a little—let people know I am here.

MRS. CRICKET. [*Singing*]
> And 'Cricket, cricket, cricket,
>   You pretty little thing . . .'

MR. CRICKET. I must get some introductions, fix up orders, have a look round. Give me the rattle, I'll use it on my way.

MRS. CRICKET. And what about me? I want it.

MR. CRICKET. Very well, darling.

MRS. CRICKET. You won't leave me long——

MR. CRICKET. Rattle for me if you want me. And I expect a neighbour will be coming along. Have a chat with him, about the children, and all that, you know.

MRS. CRICKET. You bad boy.

MR. CRICKET. Now, darling, be careful. Won't be long, my pet.   [*Runs off*

MRS. CRICKET. [*Rattles*] Hush-a-bye—cricket—on the tree top! Cricket! I feel frightened.

TRAMP. Don't you be frightened, mum. You'll 'ave an easier time than most ladies, by the look of yer.

MRS. CRICKET. Who's there, a beetle?—You don't bite?

TRAMP. No.

MRS. CRICKET. And how are the children?

TRAMP.   Ah—now you're askin'! Rum, 'ow
Yer question 'urts me, some'ow;
For, beg your pardon, Madam—
Fact is, I've never 'ad 'em.

MRS. CRICKET. Oh, dear, haven't you any children? That's a pity. [*Shakes rattle*] Cricket! Cricket! And why did you never marry, beetle?

TRAMP.   Well, some's too selfish, maybe,
To want a wife and baby . . .
Oh, 'strewth, what do I care now?—
She wouldn't 'ave me! There now.

MRS. CRICKET. Yes! Yes! You men *are* troublesome. [*Rattles*] Cricket! Cricket! Cricket!

CHRYSALIS.   In me, in me, in me,
The future strives to be!

TRAMP. Oh, buck up!

CHRYSALIS. I will accomplish such deeds.

Enter MRS. BEETLE

MRS. BEETLE. Isn't my husband here? Oh, the stupid man. Where is our pile?

MRS. CRICKET. Your pile? Can we play with it? Do let me see it.

MRS. BEETLE. It's nothing to play with, it's our future, our nest-egg, our capital. My husband, the clumsy creature, has gone off with it.

MRS. CRICKET. Oh dear, I hope he hasn't run away from you.

MRS. BEETLE. And where is yours?

MRS. CRICKET. He's away on business. Cricket! Cricket!

MRS. BEETLE. Fancy him leaving you all alone like that poor thing, and you—[*Whispers*]—aren't you?

MRS. CRICKET. Oh dear!

MRS. BEETLE. So young, too. And aren't you making a pile?

MRS. CRICKET. What for?

MRS. BEETLE. A pile—for you and him and your family. That's for your future—for your whole life.

MRS. CRICKET. Oh no, all I want is to have my own little home, my nest, a little house of my very own. And curtains, and children, and my Cricket. That's all.

MRS. BEETLE. How can you live without a pile?

MRS. CRICKET. What should I do with it?

MRS. BEETLE. Roll it about with you everywhere. There's nothing like a pile for holding a man.

MRS. CRICKET. Oh no, a little house.

MRS. BEETLE. A pile, I tell you.

MRS. CRICKET. A little house.

MRS. BEETLE. Pretty little innocence! I'd like to stay with you, but I must be going.

MRS. CRICKET. And I wanted to hear all about your children.

MRS. BEETLE. I don't want to bother over no children. My pile, that's all I want, my pile!   [*Exit*

MRS. CRICKET. Oh, what an old frump! I don't wonder her husband's run away from her. [*Sings a snatch of the song*] I've such a queer feeling. Snip! Snap! That's what he did to him—Snip!

ICHNEUMON FLY enters

ICHNEUMON FLY. Ha, ha! [*He murders* MRS. CRICKET *and drags her to his lair.*]

TRAMP. Oh, murder!

ICHNEUMON FLY. Daughter, daughter! Chicken! [*Singing*] 'Open your mouth and shut your eyes and see what some one'll send you.'

TRAMP. 'E's killed 'er, and I stood like a bloomin' log! Didn't utter a sound she didn't and nobody ran to 'elp her!

Enter PARASITE

PARASITE. Bravo! Comrade, just what I was thinking.

TRAMP. To die—like that—so young, so 'elpless.

PARASITE. Just what I was thinking. I was looking on all the time. I wouldn't do a thing like that, you know. I wouldn't really. Every one wants to live, don't they?

TRAMP. Who are you?

PARASITE. I, oh nothing much, I'm a poor man, an orphan. They call me a parasite.

TRAMP. How can any one dare to kill like that!

PARASITE. That's just what I say. Do you think he needs it? Do you think he's hungry like me? Not a bit of it. He kills to add to his larder, what's three-quarters full already. He collects things, he does, hangs 'em up to dry, smokes 'em, pickles 'em. It's a scandal, that's what it is, a scandal. One's got a store while another's starving. Why should he have a dagger, and me only my bare fists to fight with, and all over chilblains too—aren't I right?

TRAMP. I should say so.

PARASITE. There's no equality, that's what I say. One a law for the rich—another for the poor! And if I was to kill anything, I couldn't eat it—not satisfactorily, I can't chew properly, my jaw's too weak. Is that right?

TRAMP. I don't 'old with killin', no'ow.

PARASITE. My very words. Comrade, or at least, hoarding shouldn't be allowed. Eat your fill and 'ave done with it. Down with larders! Storing things is robbin' those who haven't nowhere to store. Eat your fill and have done with it and then there'd be enough for all, wouldn't there?

TRAMP. *I* dunno——

PARASITE. Well, I'm tellin' yer, aren't I? Down with——

ICHNEUMON FLY. [*Re-entering*] Eat it up baby, eat it up. Choose what you like. Have you got a nice daddy? Eh?

PARASITE. Good afternoon, my lord.

ICHNEUMON FLY. How d'ye do? Edible? [*Sniffing.*]

PARASITE. Oh no, you're joking, guv'nor, why me?

ICHNEUMON FLY. Get out, you filthy creature. What d'ye want here, clear off.

PARASITE. I'm movin', your worship; no offence, captain. [*Cowers.*]

147

ICHNEUMON FLY. [*To* TRAMP] Well, did you see that neat piece of work, eh? It's not every one who could do that. Ah, my boy, that's what you want—brains, expert knowledge, enterprise, imagination, initiative—and love of work, let me tell you.

PARASITE. That's what I say.

ICHNEUMON FLY. My good man, if you want to keep alive, you've got to fight your way. There's your future, there's your family. And then you know there must be a certain amount of ambition. A strong personality is bound to assert itself.

PARASITE. Thàt's what I say, sir.

ICHNEUMON FLY. Of course, of course. Make your way in the world. Use the talent that's in you, that's what I call a useful life.

PARASITE. Absolutely, your grace 'its it every time.

ICHNEUMON FLY. Hold your tongue, you filthy creature. I'm not talking to you.

PARASITE. No, of course you weren't, my lord, beg your pardon, I'm sure.

ICHNEUMON FLY. And how it cheers you up when you do your duty like that. 'Do the job that's nearest, though it's dull at whiles.' When you feel that, you feel that you are not living in vain. 'Life is *real*, life is earnest, life is not an empty dream,' Well, good afternoon, sir, I must be off again! 'The daily round, the common task!' So long! [*Exit*

PARASITE. The old murderer. Believe me, it was all I could do not to fly at his throat! Yes, sir, I'll work too if need be, but why should I work when somebody else has more than he can consume? I've got initiative—

but I keep it here. [*Pats stomach*] I'm 'ungry, that's what I am, 'ungry, that's a pretty state of things, isn't it?

TRAMP. Anything for a piece of meat.

PARASITE. That's what I say. Anything for a piece of meat, and the poor man's got nothing. It's against nature. Every one should have enough to eat, eh? Down with work!

TRAMP. [*Shaking rattle*] Poor creature, poor creature!

PARASITE. That's it. Every one's got a right to live.
                              [*Rattle and chirping in reply*

MR. CRICKET. [*Enters, rattling*] Here I am, my pet, here I am, my darling. Where are you, my precious? Guess what hubby's brought you.

ICHNEUMON FLY. [*Behind him*] Aha!

TRAMP. Look out—look out!

PARASITE. Don't interfere, mate—don't get mixed up in it. What must be, must be.

MR. CRICKET. Mummy!

ICHNEUMON FLY. [*Kills him*] Larva, look what your kind daddy's bringing you now.

TRAMP. Oh, Gawd in Heaven—'ow can you stand by and see it?

PARASITE. Just what I say. That's the third cricket he's had already, and me nothing. And that's what we poor working men are asked to put up with.

ICHNEUMON FLY. [*Re-entering*] No, no, kiddy, I've no time. Daddy must go back to work. Eat, eat, eat. Quiet now, I'll be back in an hour.   [*Exit*

PARASITE. It's more than I can stand—dirty old profiteer! What injustice! I'll show 'im, that I will. Just you wait! [*Trembling*] 'E's not coming back, is 'e? Keep cave! I must just 'ave a look.

TRAMP. Thank 'eaven! These 'eathen insec's may be vile,
But man—man's diff'rent. Folks like me an' you
Work 'ard, real 'ard, and makes our little pile . . .
Blast! I'm all mixed. *That's* what them beetles do.

It's what I say—*man* 'as ideals and dreams
And fam'ily love. 'Is purpose—put it plain—
Is keepin' up the race .. , 'Ullo, though—seems
I've got them crickets fairly on the brain.

Bold—that's what man is; resolute, yer might s'y.
If 'e wants more, 'e does 'is neighbour in . . .
O 'Ell! That makes 'im like this murd'rous fly . . .
But, there you are, 'oo can think straight on gin?

CHRYSALIS. I feel something great—something great.

TRAMP. What jer call great?

CHRYSALIS. To be born, to live!

TRAMP. All right, little chrysalis—I won't desert yer.

PARASITE. [*Rolling out of the* FLY'S *lair, and hiccoughing*] Ha, ha, ha! Hup—that—ha, ha, hup—the old miser— hup—kept a larder—hup—for that white-faced daughter of his. Hup—ha, ha. I feel quite—hup—I think I'm going to bust—damn the hiccoughs! It's not every one who'd eat as much as that—hup. I'm not a common man, eh, mate?

TRAMP. And 'ow about the Larva?

PARASITE. Oh, I've gobbled her up too, hup. For what we 'ave received may the—hup.

TRAMP. Gah! Bleedin' Bolshie!

ACT III
THE ANTS

TRAMP. It's like this 'ere ... What's wrong about
Them insec's, if yer think it out,
Is, they've no feller-feelin'. Each
Jest for 'isself is what *they* preach.

CHRYSALIS. Listen to me, listen to me—
The whole world will soon be free!

TRAMP. Thinks 'e's the world, 'e does ... My 'at!
These insec's all b'aves like that—
Ridic'lous creatures! Jest can't see
'Ow small they looks to you and me ...
They make me tired. ... I'd give my clay
(Gospel, I would) to get away.
Man! These 'ere insec's never dream
Of workin' to some general scheme.

CHRYSALIS. The crowning hour approaches. Lo
The universe begins to glow!

TRAMP. [*Jumping up*]
Gorblimey, if I 'aven't struck
The truth! Now, there's a bit o' luck.
Insec's won't work together. Man
Will. 'E can form a general plan.
There's something great in 'im what fights
And perishes for the nation's rights.
                                        [*Sits down*

CHRYSALIS. My wings are coming. See, they spread
Beyond the vast suns overhead!

TRAMP. I've 'it it! That's what makes men great—
Givin' their lives up for the State! ...
Man's not 'alf noble—put it straight!

'Ere, what's that bitin' me? Blimey, there's another of 'em—S'truth, I've sat on an Ant heap—'undreds and thousands—that's what they are playing at—'undreds and thousands!

[*In the meantime the Curtain rises and displays the Ant Heap. In the centre sits a* BLIND ANT *who counts continuously:* ANTS *with sacks, beans, shovels, etc., run across in time to his counting*]

BLIND ANT. One, two, three, four—one, two, three, four.

TRAMP. What's that? What yer counting for, old boy?

BLIND ANT. One, two, three, four——

TRAMP. What's this 'ere? A warehouse or a factory, isn't it? Hi, what's it for?

BLIND ANT. One, two, three, four——

TRAMP. What's this factory for, I'm asking—why's this blind feller countin'? Ah, he's giving them the time. They all move in time as he counts, one, two, three, four. Like machines—Bah, it makes my head swim,

BLIND ANT. One, two, three, four——

Enter CHIEF ENGINEER

CHIEF ENGINEER. Quicker, quicker, one, two three, four——

BLIND ANT. [*More quickly*] One, two, three, four—one, two, three, four.
[*They all move more quickly*]

TRAMP. What's that? I'm asking yer, sir, what's this 'ere factory?

CHIEF ENGINEER. What's your business?

TRAMP. Business?

CHIEF ENGINEER. From which of the Ants?

TRAMP. I'm a human man, that's what I am. Ants indeed!

CHIEF ENGINEER. This is an Ant realm. What do you want here?

TRAMP. 'Avin' a look.

CHIEF ENGINEER. Do you want work?

TRAMP. Shouldn't mind.

SECOND ENGINEER *rushes in*

2ND ENGINEER. A discovery! A discovery!

CHIEF ENGINEER. What is it?

2ND ENGINEER. A new method of speeding up. Don't count one, two, three, four—count *blank*, two, three, four—blind fellow, hullo!

BLIND ANT. One, two, three, four——

2ND ENGINEER. Wrong: Blank, two, three, four.

BLIND ANT. Blank, two, three, four. Blank, two, three, four—[ALL *move more quickly*.]

TRAMP. Not so fast—Makes me feel giddy.

2ND ENGINEER. Who are you?

TRAMP. Stranger in these parts!

2ND ENGINEER. Where from?

CHIEF ENGINEER. From the humans—Where's the Human Ant Heap?

TRAMP. What?

CHIEF ENGINEER. Where's the Human Ant Heap?

TRAMP. Oh, over there, and over there. Everywhere.

2ND ENGINEER. Ha, ha! Everywhere! Fool!

CHIEF ENGINEER. Are there any humans?

TRAMP. Yes. They're called the lords of creation, that's
what they're called.

2ND ENGINEER. Ha, ha! Lords of creation!

CHIEF ENGINEER. We are the lords of creation.

2ND ENGINEER. Ha, ha! Masters of the world!

CHIEF ENGINEER. We're the masters of the world.

2ND ENGINEER. The Ant Realm!

CHIEF ENGINEER. The largest Ant State!

2ND ENGINEER. A World Power!

CHIEF ENGINEER. The largest Democracy!

TRAMP. What's that?

CHIEF ENGINEER. The world must obey us!

2ND ENGINEER. All have to work—all for *Her*.

CHIEF ENGINEER. As *She* orders.

TRAMP. Who's Her?

CHIEF ENGINEER. The whole of the State. The Nation!

TRAMP. Why, that's just the same as us! M.P.s we 'ave
and Boro' Councillors, that's democracy—'Ave yer got
Boro' Councillors?

CHIEF ENGINEER. No, we have the whole.

TRAMP. And who speaks for the whole?

2ND ENGINEER. Ha, ha! He knows nothing.

CHIEF ENGINEER. The one who orders. She who only issues commands.

2ND ENGINEER. She abides in the law—she is nowhere else.

TRAMP. And who gives you your orders?

CHIEF ENGINEER. Reason.

2ND ENGINEER. Law.

CHIEF ENGINEER. The interests of the State.

2ND ENGINEER. That's it—that's it——

TRAMP. I like that—all for the whole, and the whole for all.

CHIEF ENGINEER. For its majesty.

2ND ENGINEER. And against its enemies.

TRAMP. What's that? Against whom?

CHIEF ENGINEER. Against all.

2ND ENGINEER. We are surrounded by enemies.

CHIEF ENGINEER. We defeated the Black Ants——

2ND ENGINEER. And starved out the Brown——

CHIEF ENGINEER. And subjugated the Greys, and only the Yellows are left; we must starve out the Yellows——

2ND ENGINEER. We must starve them all out.

TRAMP. Why?

CHIEF ENGINEER. In the interests of the whole.

2ND ENGINEER. The interests of the whole are the highest.

CHIEF ENGINEER. Interests of race——

2ND ENGINEER. Industrial interests——

CHIEF ENGINEER. Colonial interests——

2ND ENGINEER. World interests——

CHIEF ENGINEER. Interests of the world.

2ND ENGINEER. Yes, yes, that's it.

CHIEF ENGINEER. All interests are the whole's.

2ND ENGINEER. Nobody may have interests but the whole.

CHIEF ENGINEER. Interests preserve the whole.

2ND ENGINEER. And wars nourish it.

TRAMP. Ah, you've warlike Ants.

2ND ENGINEER. He knows nothing.

CHIEF ENGINEER. Our Ants are the most peaceful Ants.

2ND ENGINEER. A nation of peace.

CHIEF ENGINEER. A labour State.

2ND ENGINEER. They only wish for world power——

CHIEF ENGINEER. Because they wish for world peace——

2ND ENGINEER. In the interest of their peaceable output——

CHIEF ENGINEER. And in the interests of progress.

2ND ENGINEER. In the interest of their interests, when we rule over the world.

CHIEF ENGINEER. We shall conquer time, we wish to reign over time.

TRAMP. Over what?

CHIEF ENGINEER. Time. Time is greater than space.

2ND ENGINEER. Time has never been mastered.

CHIEF ENGINEER. The master of Time will be master of all!

TRAMP. Slowly, for the love of Mike, slowly, let me think——

CHIEF ENGINEER. Speed is the master of Time.

2ND ENGINEER. The taming of time——

CHIEF ENGINEER. He who commands speed will rule over time.

2ND ENGINEER. Blank, two, three, four—blank, two, three, four——

BLIND ANT. [*More quickly*] Blank, two, three, four—blank, two——

CHIEF ENGINEER. We must quicken the speed.

2ND ENGINEER. The speed of output.

CHIEF ENGINEER. The Peace of Life——

2ND ENGINEER. Every movement must be quickened.

CHIEF ENGINEER. Shortened——

2ND ENGINEER. Calculated——

CHIEF ENGINEER. To a second——

2ND ENGINEER. To the nth of a second——

CHIEF ENGINEER. So as to save time——

2ND ENGINEER. So as to increase the output——

CHIEF ENGINEER. Work had been too slow—labour must be carried out unsparingly——

2ND ENGINEER. Ruthlessly——

TRAMP. And what's the hurry, anyway?

CHIEF ENGINEER. The interests of the whole.

2ND ENGINEER. It is a question of output—question of power.

CHIEF ENGINEER. Peaceful competition.

2ND ENGINEER. We are fighting the battle of peace.

BLIND ANT. Blank, two, three, four——

[AN OFFICIAL *approaches the* TWO ENGINEERS *and makes a report*]

TRAMP. Blank, two, three, four! Yer *must* go quicker. Why,
If I was countin', 'stead o' you, *I*'d make them vermin fly.
Quicker, quicker, quicker! We men are jest like you——
We're all for speed. I tell yer, we're countin' quicker, too;
And if we rush to ruin, we'll 'ave ourselves to thank——
So wake up, ole blind feller. On with yer countin'! Blank——

BLIND ANT. Two, three, four——

CHIEF ENGINEER. Faster—faster——
[AN ANT *collapses with his load and moans*]

2ND ENGINEER. Tut, tut! What's that? Get up.

ANOTHER ANT. [*Next to him, bending over*] Dead!

CHIEF ENGINEER. One, two—carry him away, quick.

2ND ENGINEER. He died honourably in the cause of speed.

CHIEF ENGINEER. How are you lifting him? Too slowly, you're wasting time. Drop him. Now head and feet together. Blank, two, three—wrong, drop him again. Head and feet—blank, two, three, four—take him away—blank, two, blank, two, blank——

2ND ENGINEER. Two, three, four—quicker.

TRAMP. Anyhow, he died quick enough——

CHIEF ENGINEER. Work, work, he who possesses more, must work more.

2ND ENGINEER. He requires more——

CHIEF ENGINEER. He has more to defend——

2ND ENGINEER. And more to gain.

CHIEF ENGINEER. We are a nation of peace—peace means work.

2ND ENGINEER. And work, strength.

CHIEF ENGINEER. And strength, war.

2ND ENGINEER. Yes, yes.

Enter INVENTOR, *groping*

INVENTOR. Out of my way—step aside.

2ND ENGINEER. Our inventor——

INVENTOR. Take care, take care. Don't touch my head. It is glass, it is brittle. It is greater than I am; keep out of the way, or it will burst, smash, bang. Step aside.

2ND ENGINEER. How goes it?

INVENTOR. It hurts me, it's going to burst. It may knock against the walls—bang! I can't get my hands round it. I can scarcely carry it. Look out, do you hear? Whew, whew!

CHIEF ENGINEER. What's in it?

INVENTOR. A machine—a new machine in my head. Oh, oh, a huge machine. Out of the way, out of the way, I'm carrying a machine.

CHIEF ENGINEER. What sort of a machine?

INVENTOR. A war machine. A vast machine, a huge one. The swiftest, most effective crusher of lives. The forefront of progress, the acme of science. Whew, whew, do you hear it? Ten thousand, a hundred thousand dead! Whew, whew, it keeps on working. Two hundred thousand dead—whew, whew, whew, whew!

CHIEF ENGINEER. [*To* TRAMP] A genius, eh?

INVENTOR. Oh, oh, what pain, my head's splitting—out of the way, out of the way, don't knock against me— whew, whew, whew! [*Exit*

CHIEF ENGINEER. A vast intellect. The greatest of Scientists.

2ND ENGINEER. Nothing serves the State so much as Science.

CHIEF ENGINEER. Great is Science, and it will prevail— there will be war.

TRAMP. Why war?

CHIEF ENGINEER. Because we shall have a new war machine.

2ND ENGINEER. Because we still need a bit of the world.

CHIEF ENGINEER. A bit of the world from the Birch tree to the Pine tree.

2ND ENGINEER. The road between the two blades of grass——

CHIEF ENGINEER. The only open road to the South——

2ND ENGINEER. A question of prestige.

CHIEF ENGINEER. And trade.

2ND ENGINEER. The rights of nationality.

CHIEF ENGINEER. We or the Yellows——

2ND ENGINEER. Never was war more honourable or urgent——

CHIEF ENGINEER. Than the war we must fight.

2ND ENGINEER. We are prepared.

CHIEF ENGINEER. We have only to find a *casus belli*.

BLIND ANT. Blank, two, three, four——   *[A gong*

CHIEF ENGINEER. What's that?

VOICE. [*Outside*] A messenger! A messenger!

Enter MESSENGER

MESSENGER. I beg to announce myself. From the G.H.Q. Southern Army.

CHIEF ENGINEER. Good.

MESSENGER. In accordance with our instructions, we crossed the frontier of the Yellows——

CHIEF ENGINEER. What then?

MESSENGER. The Yellows captured me and took me to their Commander-in-Chief——

CHIEF ENGINEER. And——?

MESSENGER. Here is his letter——

CHIEF ENGINEER. Show it me. 'The Government of the Yellow Ants calls upon the Ant Realm within three months to withdraw their Army lying between the Birch tree and the Pine tree between the two blades of grass.'

2ND ENGINEER. Listen to him.

CHIEF ENGINEER. 'This territory comprises the historical, vital, industrial, general, and military interests of our State, so that it rightly belongs to us.'

2ND ENGINEER. An insult, an insult, we shall not tolerate it!

CHIEF ENGINEER. 'Meanwhile we are giving orders to our Army to mobilize.' War, war, at last!

2ND ENGINEER. At last a war is forced upon us.

CHIEF ENGINEER. To arms!

ANOTHER MESSENGER *runs on*

2ND MESSENGER. The Yellows are marching across our frontier——

CHIEF ENGINEER. To arms! To arms!

2ND MESSENGER. Mobilization—to arms!

BOTH MESSENGERS. To arms! To arms!
[*Alarm sirens—from all sides the* ANTS *scramble into the* ANT HEAP]

BLIND ANT. Blank, two, three, four—blank, two, three, four——
[*Increasing din within*]

TRAMP. It does yer good to see 'em pass,
   Prepared to shed their blood——
   An'd jest for 'alf a yard o' mud,
  Between two blades o' grass.

  It does yer good to see 'em all
   So 'andsome and so spry.
   They're not afraid to up and die——

They've 'eard the Nation's call.

It makes yer think o' them ole scenes,
    With star-shells over 'ead,
    The night we left a thousan' dead——

And keptured two latrines.
Now, fellers, dig yerselves right in,
    And stay there till yer bust.
    Them Yellers wants your yard o' dust,
And don't you let 'em win!

CHRYSALIS. They call, they shout, they beat their drums.
        The world wakes. The great moment comes!

[*Beating of drums*—ANTS *transform themselves into*
SOLDIERS. CHIEF ENGINEER *becomes* COMMAN-
DER-IN-CHIEF]

TRAMP. Now, that's what trainin' does. You're smart
        lads. Put it there!
    Crumbs! If you're half the ant I takes yer for, I
        swear
    You'll cop that bit o' land afore the Yellers cop
        it——
    But 'ere's the brass 'ats comin'. I guess I'd better
        'op it.

CHIEF ENGINEER. Soldiers! We find ourselves compelled
to call you to the colours. A wicket enemy has treacher-
ously attacked us, for the purpose of outwitting our
peaceable preparations. At this great hour I have been
appointed Dictator.

2ND ENGINEER. Three cheers for the Dictator—Shout
boys, or——

SOLDIERS. Hip, hip, hooray!

CHIEF ENGINEER. [*Saluting*] Thank you! You have
responded to the gravity of the moment. Soldiers, we
are fighting for life and liberty.

2ND ENGINEER. And for the greatness of our State.

CHIEF ENGINEER. And for the greatness of our State.
We shall wage war for the interest of civilization and
our military honour. Soldiers, I am with you to the last
drop of my blood.

2ND ENGINEER. Long live our beloved Commander-in-
Chief!

SOLDIERS. Long live our Commander-in-Chief!

CHIEF ENGINEER. I know my soldiers. They will fight
until the final victory. Long live our gallant men.
Hurrah!

SOLDIERS. Hurrah! Hurrah!

CHIEF ENGINEER. [*To* 2ND ENGINEER] The First and
Second Divisions will attack frontally. The Fourth will
envelop the Pine Wood, and break into the Ant Heap
of the Yellows. Women and children to be slaughtered
—Third Division in reserve—no quarter!

[SECOND ENGINEER *salutes*]

May God assist us in this. Soldiers, 'shun! Right turn—
quick march!

[*Drums*]

One, two! War forced upon us—one, two, one, two! In
the name of Justice! No quarter! For your hearths and
homes! One, two, one, two! We are only defending
ourselves. War on the world. For a Greater Home
Country. One, two—a ruthless enemy. Will of the
Nation! To battle—strike hard. Historical claims.
Brilliant spirit of the Army. One, two, one, two!

[*Fresh* TROOPS *march past*]

Good luck, soldiers, I shall be behind you—Well done
the Fifth! The conquerors of the Pine Trees. A mighty
epoch, to victory—conquer the world, magnificent

daring—one, two! Well done, Seventh! Beat them, soldiers, the Yellows are cowards. Hack your way through, burn, destroy, heroes!

Enter MESSENGER

MESSENGER. The Yellows have invaded the stretch of country between the roots of the Pine Tree and the Stone——

CHIEF ENGINEER. Entirely according to plan. Faster, soldiers, one, two. War forced on us for honour and glory, needs of the State, no conception of Justice; soldiers, show your bravery, victory is ours, greatest moment in history. Quick march, quick march, quick march!
    [*Big bang in the distance*]
The battle is beginning. Up with the reserves.
    [*Looks through the telescope*]

BLIND ANT. Blank, two, three, four—blank——
    [*Increasing din*]

CHRYSALIS. Wild voices of the world, be dumb!
    Your woes are at an end. I come!

CHIEF ENGINEER. Reserves, stand to! [*To* 2ND ENGINEER] Issue a report.

2ND ENGINEER. [*In a loud voice*] The battle has begun at last, under favourable weather conditions. Our heroic men are fighting in magnificent spirits.

CHIEF ENGINEER. Right turn, quick march!—one, two, one, two—faster boys!

Enter MESSENGER

MESSENGER. Our right wing is retreating. The Fifth Regiment is completely destroyed.

CHIEF ENGINEER. According to plan. Sixth Regiment, replace them.

TRAMP. Ho, yuss! ... There was other reports that began
    'The Regiment was butchered—accordin' to plan!'
    And after 'is battle, 'e'll go round and scan
    The corpses, all 'eaped up—'accordin' to plan'.

Enter STRETCHER-BEARERS *with wounded*

A WOUNDED MAN. The Fifth Regiment, our regiment—we're all destroyed. Stop! Stop!
[*Telegraph instrument clatters*]

SIGNAL OFFICER. [*Reading dispatch*] 'Fifth Regiment destroyed. We await orders.'

CHIEF ENGINEER. Sixth, take its place. [*To* 2ND ENGINEER] Issue a report.

2ND ENGINEER. The battle is developing successfully. The Fifth Regiment especially distinguished itself, heroically repelling all attacks, whereupon it was relieved by the Sixth.

CHIEF ENGINEER. Bravo! I will decorate you with the Steel Cross.

2ND ENGINEER. Thank you. I am only doing my duty.

JOURNALIST. [*Approaching with note-book*] I am a journalist; shall we announce a victory?

CHIEF ENGINEER. Yes. Successful operations. Thanks to our plans prepared years ago. The admirable spirit of our forces—irresistible advance—the enemy demoralized.

JOURNALIST. We—we—we——

CHIEF ENGINEER. Eh?

JOURNALIST. We will print everything.

CHIEF ENGINEER. Good. We rely upon the co-operation of the Press. Don't forget the admirable spirit.

JOURNALIST. The Press is performing its d-duty!

[*Exit*

Enter PHILANTHROPIST *with collecting-box*

PHILANTHROPIST. Help the wounded! All for the wounded! Gifts for the wounded. Give to the wounded. Help for the cripples.

CHIEF ENGINEER. Second Division, attack—it must break through whatever the sacrifice.

PHILANTHROPIST. For our heroes—help your brothers —help for the wounded.

TRAMP. War for the wounded! Coppers for their wounds.

PHILANTHROPIST. Help for the wounded—give to the cripples.

TRAMP. [*He tears off a button and puts it in the collecting-box*] All for the wounded! My last button for the war!

ANOTHER WOUNDED MAN. Oh! Put me out of my misery, do!

PHILANTHROPIST. Aid the wounded.

[*Telegraph instrument again*]

SIGNAL OFFICER. The right wing of the Yellows is retreating.

CHIEF ENGINEER. Pursue them. Finish them off. Don't bother about prisoners.

2ND ENGINEER. The enemy retiring in confusion. Our

regiments in defiance of death, dogging his footsteps with splendid daring.

CHIEF ENGINEER. Fourth Levy!

SIGNAL OFFICER. The Fourth Regiment has invested the Pine Tree and has made a rear attack on the Ant Heap of the Yellows—the garrison is slaughtered.

CHIEF ENGINEER. Raze it to the ground—finish off the civilians.

SIGNAL OFFICER. The enemy is overwhelmed—they have evacuated a foot of the furze bush.

CHIEF ENGINEER. Victory is ours. [*Falls on knees and removes his helmet*] Great god of the Ants, thou hast granted victory to thy servants. I appoint thee honorary Colonel. [*Jumps up*] Third Division, forward, all reserves forward—no prisoners. Forward! [*Again on his knees*] Righteous god of strength, thou knowest that our holy cause—[*Jumps up*] After them—after them— attack them—hunt them down—slaughter everybody. The empire of the world is settled. [*Kneels*] God of the Ants, in this significant hour—[*Prays silently.*]

TRAMP. [*Bending over him softly*] Empire of the World! You miserable Ant you, you call this bit of clay and grass the world? This dirty little patch of soil? If I was to trample down all this 'ere Ant 'eap of yours and you with it, d'yer think these 'ere trees above yer would notice it? Not they!

CHIEF ENGINEER. Who are you?

TRAMP. Only a voice. Though yesterday p'r'aps I was a soldier on another ant heap. What yer think of yerself, conqueror of the world? Feel big enough? Don't that 'eap of corpses seem too small—for your glory, yer miserable image?

CHIEF ENGINEER. [*Rising*] I disregard you entirely—I proclaim myself Emperor!

SIGNAL OFFICER. The Second Division is asking for reinforcements. Our troops seem exhausted.

CHIEF ENGINEER. They must hold out. Shoot down defaulters.

SIGNAL OFFICER. The Third Division has been thrown into confusion.

AN ANT. [*Escapes across stage*] We're running away!

CHIEF ENGINEER. Mobilize the nation!

A SHOUT. No! No! Back, back!

PIERCING CRY. Save yourselves!

CHIEF ENGINEER. Send the unfit to the front—ever one must go!

SOLDIER. They're beating us, run.

TWO SOLDIERS. They've surrounded us—escape!

A SOLDIER. To the West. Escape to the West!

SOLDIERS. They've surrounded us from the West—run to the East!

CHIEF ENGINEER. Back! To your places—to the front. Face to West.

CROWD. [*From* R.] Escape—they're hunting us down. To the East.

CROWD. [*From* L.] To the West, out of the way, they're here!
     [*The two streams begin to fight*]

CHIEF ENGINEER. [*Shouting at them*] Back, cowards! You cattle—I am your Emperor.

A SOLDIER. Lie down. [*Runs him through*] Escape!

2ND ENGINEER. [*Runs in wounded*] They've taken the city. Put out the lights.

THE YELLOWS. [*Penetrating from both sides*] Hurrah! Hurrah! The Ant Heap is ours!
    [*Lights go out: confusion*]

2ND ENGINEER. Fight! Fight! Ah!

YELLOW LEADER. Into the passages after them—spare nobody, slaughter all the men.

SHOUTS OF SLAUGHTERMEN. Ah! Ah!

BLIND ANT. Blank, two—blank, two—blank, two.

YELLOW LEADER. After them—murder—murder them all.
    [*The din becomes more remote*]

BLIND ANT. Blank, two—blank, two—blank, two——

YELLOW LEADER. Light!
    [*Lights are lit—the foreground is empty—corpses piled everywhere*]
Excellent, Yellows. All are slaughtered.

TRAMP. Chuck it, General!

YELLOW LEADER. The victory of the Yellows. The victory of justice and progress. Ours is the path between the two blades of grass. The world belongs to us Yellows. I proclaim myself Ruler of the Universe.

CHRYSALIS. I—I—I——

YELLOW LEADER. [*On his knees*] Most righteous god of the Ants—thou knowest that we fight only for justice, our victory, our national honour, our commercial interests.

TRAMP. [*Rushes out, kicks him over, and grinds him into pieces with his boot*] Bah! Yer insec', yer insec'!

EPILOGUE

DEATH AND LIFE

SCENE: *Interior of the forest. Pitch-black night. The* TRAMP *sleeping in the foreground.*

TRAMP. [*Speaking in his sleep*] Chuck it, General! [*Wakes*] Been nappin', 'ave I? Crumbs, I feel cold. I'm sick—shiverin' all over ... Where am I? Can't see me 'ands, it's so bloomin' dark ... 'Oo's that speakin'? ... [*Shouting*] 'Ullo! 'oo's talkin'? ... Nothin'—no one anywhere. Gawd! I'm skeered. Where's the sky got to? There ain't no sky! Can't be dead, can I? Feel sick enough. For 'eaven's sake, a bit of light—just a glimmer!

A VOICE. Wait, wait. The light is coming.

TRAMP. I can 'ear voices—everywhere, voices! 'Ark!

VOICE OF ANT-SOLDIER. I'm wounded ... I'm thirsty.

VOICE OF ANT-COMMANDER. Army of Occupation, advance!

VOICE OF MR. BEETLE. My pile! Where's my little pile?

VOICE OF A BUTTERFLY. Iris! Iris!

TRAMP. Give us a bit of light! I'm skeered!

VOICE OF CRICKET. Another cricket lived here a long time ago. Careful, mumsy, careful!

VOICE OF ICHNEUMON FLY. Aha! Got them!

VOICE OF ANT-SOLDIER. Water, water!

VOICE OF ANT-COMMANDER. And see that you take no prisoners.

VOICE OF A BUTTERFLY. Iris! Iris!

VOICE OF MR. BEETLE. My pile! Where's my lovely pile?

TRAMP. What's 'ere? A flint! If only I could strike a spark from it, jest one, one little spark o' light!

> [*He strikes it upon another stone. Sparks burst forth. The forest is lit up*]

Thank 'eaven, 'ere's light!

VOICES. Escape! escape!

CHRYSALIS. Who is that calling me? I come. I come!
[MUSIC]
> My wings begin to sever:
> My outer sheath is torn . . .

VOICES OF MOTHS. [*Rapidly coming near and nearer*]
Into it, into it, into it! Wing your flight
Into the ecstasy, into the heart of the light!

CHRYSALIS. I shall have life for ever;
> I shall at last be born!

> [MOTHS *in a bevy fly into the midst of the light. They whirl round*]

MOTHS. Into it, into it, into it! Wing your flight
Into the ecstasy, into the heart of the light!

TRAMP. What are *you*? Moths? What yer want? Is it life?

FIRST MOTH. [*Separating from the others*] Ah . . . ! [*Stands still*]
> We are struck from the dark
> And again we expire.
> Each is a spark
> Of an infinite fire. . . .

> [*She falls dead*]

CHORUS. And to flash from the forge for a moment, and perish, is all our desire.

TRAMP. Why's she dead? She didn't want to die.

SECOND MOTH. [*Separating, etc.*] Ah . . . ! [*Stands still*]

> We are drops on the crest
> Of a fountain that leaps——

[*she falls dead*]

THIRD MOTH. [*Separating*]

> We dance without rest
> And return to the deeps,——

CHORUS. For life is eternal, and rises from death where you think that it sleeps.

THIRD MOTH. Life is eternal. It cannot fail.
> All hail to life——

[*Falls dead*

MOTHS. All hail, all hail!

TRAMP. Life and death—seems they're both good if we know how to treat 'em. I'm a battered old moth, I am, but I'll dance with yer! All hail to life!

MOTHS. All hail, all hail!

[MOTH *after* MOTH *falls dead*]

TRAMP. Butterflies, beetles, moths, and men—why can't we all live 'appy together? The world's big enough, and life could be 'appy for everythink—if we 'ad a bit o' sense.

MOTHS. All hail, all hail!

CHRYSALIS. [*Shrieking*] Out of my way! Behold!
[*She rends her husk and leaps forth as a* MOTH]

TRAMP. What? You, Chrysalis? Reely born?

CHRYSALIS-MOTH. [*Whirling*] Ah! [*Stands still*]

> O light! O love! O ecstasy
> Of being! Life has entered *me*!

A FEW LAST MOTHS. Eternal life—all hail to thee!

> [*They fall dead*]

CHRYSALIS-MOTH.

> Hearken, O heaven! O earth, give ear!
> I will proclaim a mystery here.
> I will solve all things. I will tell
> The whole world's meaning. Hearken well. . . .
>
> [*She falls dead*]

TRAMP. [*Kneeling by the dead* CHRYSALIS] Dead. She's dead too. Pore Chrysalis—and you 'ad sich 'opes. What was yer going to say? I wonder! They don't seem skeered o' death, these little mites don't. Life's a rapture to them, and death's a rapture. It's queer. Pore little mites—all done for. . . . 'Ere—what's this? My turn, is it? Get off my chest, damn yer! I won't die. 'Aven't I jest learned 'ow to live and let live? Gawd, I feel sick. I can't be dyin'? It can't 'ave come to me? . . . Chuck it—yer stranglin' me. I know 'oo it is—you're Death. Yer want to count me out—*I* know. Take that!

Enter TWO SNAILS

FIRST SNAIL. Thtop—Thome one's makin' a noith.

SECOND SNAIL. Come back, come back.

TRAMP. That's for you, rattlebones! You felt that, eh? 'Ere, get yer knee off my chest—I only want to live. I won't give yer my life, yer old skull and crossbones yer —Ow! it's 'is foot on my head.

> [*Falls*]

FIRST SNAIL. I thay, thnail.

SECOND SNAIL. What?

FIRST SNAIL. 'E'th thtruggling with death.

SECOND SNAIL. We'll have a look, eh?

TRAMP. Let me live—what will it matter to you? Only this once—till tomorrow. Let me breathe—stop, don't strangle me—I don't want to die—I 'aven't enjoyed life yet—not 'alf——

    [*Falls*]

FIRST SNAIL. What fun, eh?

SECOND SNAIL. I thay, thnail!

FIRST SNAIL. What?

SECOND SNAIL. He'th done for.

TRAMP. You strangle a man when 'e's down, do you, coward? Stop, let me tell you—all I want's another moment—let me live—go away—I've more to tell you —I've learned how to live.

FIRST SNAIL. Well, it'th all up with him.

SECOND SNAIL. Oh dear, oh dear! What a mithfortune! How we shall mith him, my dear.

FIRST SNAIL. What are you talkin' about? It's nothing to do with uth.

SECOND SNAIL. That's what people thay when thome-body dies.

FIRST SNAIL. Oh yeth. Well, we won't futh about it.

SECOND SNAIL. No! No! Ith the way of the world.

    [*Dawn*—BIRDS *awaken*]

    Enter WOODCUTTER

WOODCUTTER. [*Singing*]
    'As I went down to Shrewsbury Town
    I came by luck . . .'
[*He sees the* TRAMP'S *corpse*] Hallo—what's this?
Boozed, is he? Here—wake up, mate. My word! he's
dead. Poor old chap. . . . Well, anyway, he'll have no
more trouble.

    Enter a WOMAN, *carrying a new-born baby*

WOMAN. Morning, Peter Wood. Why, whatever's the
matter?
    [*Church bells*]

WOODCUTTER. He's dead.

WOMAN. Dead? Who is it?

WOODCUTTER. Only a tramp by the look of him.

WOMAN. It gives me a turn. It's bad luck, you know.
Here am I taking my sister's baby to be baptized, and—
ugh!

WOODCUTTER. One's born and another dies. No great
matter, missus.

WOMAN. It means bad luck.

WOODCUTTER. What's death? There's always people
enough. [*Chucking the baby under the chin*] Gi-gi-gi-gigg,
baby! Wait till you're grown up!

WOMAN. I hope he'll be better off than we are, that's all.
These taxes!

WOODCUTTER. Plenty of work—that's what he'll need.
    [*Voices of* SCHOOL CHILDREN *approaching*]

WOMAN. Here come the girls on their way to school.
Quick, Peter Wood—cover up that! They mustn't see
it, poor dears.

Enter some SCHOOL CHILDREN. *They file across the
stage singing:*

'As I went down to Shrewsbury Town,
I came by luck on a silver crown:
  And what shall I buy with that, said I,
What shall I buy in Shrewsbury Town?

As I went down to Shrewsbury Town,
I saw my love in a dimity gown:
  And all so gay I gave it away,
I gave it away—my silver crown.'

[*During the song one little girl gives a flower to the baby.
This, after the singers have left the stage, the* WOMAN
takes and lays on the body of the TRAMP]

CURTAIN

Act I

6-7 Story of old Rossum

9 The Nature of Robots

16 - Management enterprise sexually frustrating

21 - Humanity League - liberating the Robots

23 - Robots epilepsy - need for pain

25 - Domain's vision of the future - no work

26 - Alquist's objections - dignity of labor.
   cooking preparations

28 - Robot sex
   Domain proposes

Act II

32 - Emma's attitude to Robots - "worse than anims"

33 - Robots as unnatural

37 - Offstage developments - robots used in war

40 - Robot manifesto - organisation

43 - Alquist's prayer - against progress

44 - Radius - superior Robot

48 - Man dying out due to competitive
   influence of profit motive - Robots continue
   to be manufactured

50 - Burning of plans - female act - return to
   Nature

54 - bourgeois reaction to crisis - abandon ship
   Helman's faith in "the time-table"

57 - Domain's new plans - National Robots

OXFORD

MORE OXFORD PAPERBACKS

Details of a selection of other books follow. A complete list of Oxford Paperbacks, including The World's Classics, Twentieth-Century Classics, OPUS, Past Masters, Oxford Authors, Oxford Shakespeare, and Oxford Paperback Reference, is available in the UK from the General Publicity Department, Oxford University Press (JN), Walton Street, Oxford OX2 6DP.

In the USA, complete lists are available from the Paperbacks Marketing Manager, Oxford University Press, 200 Madison Avenue, New York, NY 10016.

Oxford Paperbacks are available from all good bookshops. In case of difficulty, customers in the UK can order direct from Oxford University Press Bookshop, 116 High Street, Oxford, Freepost, OX1 4BR, enclosing full payment. Please add 10 per cent of published price for postage and packing.

Act III

66 - Domain & Alquist argue over causes

67 - Domain's ideals - Marx?
Questioning of motive - work/profit/

69 - Alquist's accusations of enjoyment guilt

70 - Dr Gall's ambition - changed Robots

71 - Revolution Helena's fault for wanting robots to have souls

74 - Berman blames demand for robots

77 - Dream of beginning over again

DIMETOS AND TWO EARLY PLAYS

Athol Fugard

'Dimetos had a guilty love for his niece, who hanged herself. One day the waves carried on to the fine sand of the beach mthe body of a marvellously beautiful young woman. Seeing her, Dimetos fell on his knees, stricken with love. But he was forced to watch the decay of this magnificent body, and went mad. This was the niece's vengeance, and the symbol of a condition we must try to define.' In this paragraph from the Notebooks of Albert Camus, lies the imaginative kernel of Athol Fugard's play *Dimetos*. The two early plays, *No-Good Friday* and *Nongogo* are both for chiefly black casts. In *No-Good Friday*, the hero is compelled by circumstance to take action against the forces of corruption which threaten to engulf his personality and undermine his integrity. In *Nongogo* Queeny, shebeen-owner and former prostitute, meets honest, hardworking Johnny, and we witness the mutual impact of their opinions about themselves and each other. These plays exhibit Fugard's characteristic compassion, fierceness, dissatisfaction, and humour.

FOUR MAJOR PLAYS

Henrik Ibsen

Translated by James McFarlane and Jens Arup

Introduced by James McFarlane

The four plays in this World's Classics volume are *A Doll's House*, *Ghosts*, *Hedda Gabler*, and *The Master Builder*.

The World's Classics

THE CONCISE OXFORD COMPANION TO THE THEATRE

Edited by Phyllis Hartnoll

The Concise Oxford Companion to the Theatre is an essential handbook for the theatre-goer or the drama student. It contains entries on actors and actresses from Sarah Bernhardt to Alec McCowen; on theatrical companies and theatre buildings from the Abbey Theatre in Dublin to the Yvonne Arnaud Theatre in Guildford; and on dramatists from Sophocles to Samuel Beckett. The range of the volume is international, and also includes explanations of technical terms, and notes on practical and historical aspects of stagecraft and design.

For this concise version, based on Phyllis Hartnoll's third edition of *The Oxford Companion to the Theatre*, each article has been considered afresh, and most have been recast and rewritten, often with the addition of new material.

Oxford Paperback Reference

SELECTED PLAYS

Athol Fugard

'New introduction by Dennis Walder

'Master Harold' . . . and the boys
Hello and Goodbye
Blood Knot (New Version)
Boesman and Lena

Set in Port Elizabeth, South Africa, the four plays in this selection of Fugard's best work explore close and tense family relationships against a background of wider suffering and tensions, engaging our sympathies for South Africans of all races in their struggle to retain dignity and hope. The volume marks the first publication of a new version of one of Fugard's finest plays, *Blood Knot*.

'Fugard is the sole dramatist now writing in English whose plays contain the necessary dualism of true tragedy.' John Elsom in the *Listener*

BOESMAN AND LENA AND OTHER PLAYS
The Blood Knot, People are Living There, Hello and Goodbye, Boesman and Lena

Athol Fugard

This is a new collection of four of Athol Fugard's best plays, which were all written in the 1960s. Some of them—in particular, *The Blood Knot*—explore the debasement of humanity which the apartheid system in South Africa encourages; but none is in any way a political manifesto. Whether portraying poor whites, Africans, or Coloureds, all the plays in this collection concentrate on the private hopes and aspirations, the instinct for survival, and the loyalties and betrayals common to all human relationships. They all admirably demonstrate the qualities of sensitivity, humour, and sense of dialogue which have made Athol Fugard one of the most widely-acclaimed dramatists writing today. Included in this collection is a long introduction by Mr Fugard which is in part a candid autobiography.

'*The Blood Knot, Hello & Goodbye, People are Living There & Boesman & Lena*—all unmistakably indigenous in their concreteness of detail & their local flavour yet universal in their recognition of the anguish of all humanity, belongs on every intelligent person's bookshelf.' *New International*

SELECTED PLAYS
Christopher Fry

This one-volume collection of some of Christopher Fry's best work includes: *The Boy with a Cart* (1939), *A Phoenix Too Frequent* (1946), *The Lady's Not for Burning* (1949), *A Sleep of Prisoners* (1951), and *Curtmantle* (1961).

'Poetic drama is always rewarding to read in its own right: particularly the work of this playwright, whose thoughtfulness in exploring themes and sensitive care for the English language make a slow savouring of his texts a particular pleasure.' *Church Times*